Don Draper

Ps 37: 4+5

John 14: 1 TO 3

Miracles at the Door

by

Don Draper

Revised Edition

phone 706~504-9192

TEACH Services, Inc.
P U B L I S H I N G
www.TEACHServices.com

Copyright © 1995, Revised 2012 TEACH Services, Inc.
ISBN-13: 978-1-57258-945-2 (Paperback)
ISBN-13: 978-1-57258-858-5 (e-Pub)
ISBN-13: 978-1-57258-859-2 (Kindle)

Library of Congress Control Number: 2012946045

Published by

TEACH Services, Inc.
P U B L I S H I N G
www.TEACHServices.com

Dedication

I 'd like to dedicate this book to Bill May, Joe Hunt, and Dave Haugsted. I would also like to thank my great district leaders who worked with me and helped me grow a lot spiritually.

Tom Chastang	Bill Boyd
Richard Atwell	Lance Morrison
Gary Bevins	Bill Fentress
John Creelman	John Mason
Woody Pangborn	

There are also many literature evangelists who have been a great inspiration to me. When I was down, they were there to talk with me and encourage me. When things got tough, we strengthened one another in prayer.

Jim and Lynne Thoreson	Len Hennlein
Larry McDaniel and family	Adam Stramel
David Furrow	Dave Tinsley
Richard Baxter	Ann Collins
Rob Gatling	Mike and Nancy Poist
Ben Johnson	Mike Bernoi

Paul Hutchins and family

Janet Lamb and family

Dale Dinterman and family

Shirley Hardy

Chris Simons and family

Tommy Hartwell

Camille Karim

Reggie Chavez

Evalynne Richardson

and many more

Editorial Consultant: Debra J. Hicks

I would also like to thank my family for supporting me in this work. Without the prayers of my wife, Sue, my son, Michael, and my daughter, Danielle, I would not have been so successful.

Table of Contents

Introduction

What a miraculous God we serve! As I leaf through the pages of my life, I clearly see how God has led through the years.

I've been a literature evangelist since 1975. During that time I've seen God work in ways that have thrilled my heart without compare. I've had the privilege of seeing many precious souls come to Christ. Knowing that I have been given this sacred opportunity to witness makes my life complete.

Literature evangelists have the significant duty of visiting in homes and sharing with people the love of Jesus. They continually see the battles people face—with Christ on one side, and Satan on the other. They see how the Holy Spirit can change lives that were once thought unchangeable.

As I look back to the years before I became a literature evangelist, I see how God worked in my life. As a young boy growing up, I didn't come from a religious-oriented home. For many years I attended church only occasionally. Then I started dating a young lady named Sue, who later became my wife, and together we attended a Methodist church. But we knew that we weren't being fed spiritually. Later, Sue's mom started searching, and God showed her the way to come into this message. She and her family, and later on my wife and I, became Seventh-day Adventists. We've been attending faithfully for the past forty-four years.

I pray that as you read this book, you'll draw closer to God. Perhaps this book will even inspire *you* to become a literature evangelist! We all want to finish this work so we can go home to heaven, don't we? God has called us to do something special for Him, and we can't let Him down.

When I ran track as a young man in high school, I would kneel down on the track and ask God to be with my team and to really bless me. I had a selfish prayer then. I prayed that He would let me win. I didn't understand God's ways. But even then He was shaping me and molding me—like the Potter and the clay. I ran more than eighty races, and many of those I won. I was called to the Olympics but turned it down. Now I know why—because God was calling me to run the greatest race of my life. It's a race that takes a lifetime, but at the end is the ultimate reward—a crown of life.

In the twelfth grade I ran against a young man named Brooks, and he was very fast. That race meant everything to me because it was my last race as a high school senior. I practiced for that race until I won it. But now, I'm running an even greater race—the greatest race in the world. As you read this book, may it help you in your race for the crown of life and an eternal home.

When I began the literature work, I'd had only three days of training with my first district leader, Tom Chastang. We sold only one book in those three days, and after that I was on my own. I prayed that if God wanted me in this work, then He'd have to show me. If not, I would quit.

I had two lead cards for addresses in Emmitsburg, Maryland. The first family I visited with was a young couple with one child. They bought the three-volume *You And Your Health* set. The second family was an older couple who bought the You And Your Health set also.

The day was coming to a close, so I started home all excited about how God had blessed. On the way home, I remembered a girl I had gone to high school with and stopped to visit her. I had a wonderful chat with Linda and her husband, and they also purchased the three-volume medical set. God had blessed me with three sales that day!

The next day when my district leader and I got together, he was shocked that I hadn't written a contract for any of the sales. I had just collected the down payment from each family, because he hadn't even showed me how to write the contract! That day we went back to all three families and wrote up the contracts. Without a doubt, I knew that God had called me to be a literature evangelist.

I Believe!

The address on the lead card was for a rural route in Thurmont, Maryland. When I asked about it at the post office, I was told to go up into the mountain area. I prayed that the Lord would help me get there because it had snowed the day before.

I went up the mountain in my little Chevy Chevette and finally came to the driveway of Mike Johnson. The driveway was a sheet of ice, but I could see that down at the bottom was a log cabin. I said a little prayer that the Lord would help me get down to his house.

When I showed Mike his lead card at the door, he invited me in. As I talked with Mike and his wife, Susie, I noticed several things around me. There were cigarettes, beer cans, and impure magazines lying around. But I thought to myself, "This would be a beautiful family to win for God."

Mike and Susie finally decided to buy a book called *Bible Readings for the Home*. I had prayer with Mike and Susie and was just about to go out the door when the Lord impressed me to ask them if they'd like to have Bible studies. Mike looked at Susie sort of funny and then said, "Sure, why not?"

We set up an appointment to begin the Bible studies the following week. At the conclusion of our first study together, Mike said, "I hope you don't mind staying the night because that driveway is so bad that I can't even get up it with my Jeep in four-wheel drive. So I don't think you're going anywhere."

I said, "Well, you don't know my God." I walked out and got in my car, and Mike was just standing there waiting to see what would happen. I started up my little Chevette and said a quick prayer, then drove right up the icy driveway.

The following week I came back for the Bible study, and this time their driveway was more icy because it had snowed again that week. I slid down and parked my car facing the hill. That night it seemed Mike could hardly wait until the study was over just to see if I could get out of his driveway!

After prayer, Mike said, "We made up an extra room because we know you'll never make it out. We've been sledding on it, and it's even worse than last week."

I just said, "Well, you don't know my God." So I started my little Chevy up, said another prayer, and drove right up and out of his driveway.

The following week I returned for the Bible study, and there was hardly any snow on the driveway; it was almost bare.

As he met me, Mike exclaimed, "I believe! I believe! There has to be a God to get you out of this driveway, because I can't even get out of it with my Jeep. I have to go up through the woods to get out, and you got up that driveway with that little Chevy Chevette. I even have four-wheel drive! I really believe that there is a God."

I just laughed and gave them the study. We had a good study that night, and when I went to leave his driveway, I got stuck. Mike had to pull me out with his Jeep. That's how God works. Sometimes He helps us through problems and errors just to show others there is a God in heaven. After Mike and Susie believed, the miracle was no longer necessary.

About a year later, with the pastor's help and plenty of Bible study and prayer, Mike and Susie were baptized. God sent me down that driveway and into that home for two precious souls who were waiting to be given the invitation.

The Blank Check

One time I was knocking on doors in Middletown, Maryland, and it seemed that the people just weren't interested. I started to wonder if I should pull out and go somewhere else to work.

Then I saw a little apartment house. Soon after I started knocking on the doors, I began to realize that only older people lived there. I didn't realize it at first, but there were two doors to each apartment. As I was knocking on one door, a lady opened the other door and asked what I wanted. We talked for a while, and then she invited me in. As we talked, she explained that she was taking care of an older lady. I began telling her about the health books, and I could tell she was very interested. When I told her the price and the amount she needed for the down payment, she told me to come to her house later that evening or the next day.

I began to pray silently that God would intervene, because many times when you go back for the down payment, the people say no and don't purchase the books. About that time, the lady remembered that she had put a blank check in her purse that morning. She checked her purse, and there it was. It just goes to show that even before you get up in the morning, God has your day planned.

Always a Reason

The postmaster in Union Bridge, Maryland, gave me directions to the address on the lead card and then told me that the man I was looking for was a minister. Just before I got to his house, I pulled over to the side of the road and said a short prayer to God. I believe this is so important because I know that God sends His angels ahead of me to prepare the hearts of the people.

As I pulled into the driveway, the minister and his son were working outdoors near their swimming pool. I showed the man the card he had sent in, and he looked a bit shocked. He told me that the handwriting wasn't his, but that it belonged to his eight-year-old son! We had a good visit and he purchased a *Steps to Christ*.

However, I had a feeling there was more in store for me since I had come so far. I stopped at the next house and was invited inside. After a short presentation, the woman who lived there purchased a small set of children's books and a *Steps to Christ*.

Some literature evangelists think that following up lead cards is a waste of time. But over the years, I've learned that every card was sent in for a reason. Even if the people themselves aren't interested, I make it my policy to visit at least two other homes in that neighborhood because it may be that God didn't send me to talk to the person who filled out the lead card, but to his next-door neighbor.

God Answers Prayer

I was working my way down toward my hometown. It was a holiday, so I knew most people would be home. My first stop was an apartment house, and at the bottom of it was a beauty salon. I discovered that I'd gone to high school with the young lady who ran it, and after showing her the health books, she decided to purchase a set.

At the next few houses I visited, the people just weren't interested. A couple of hours later I met this really tough person. After talking to him for a minute at the door, I accepted his invitation to come into the house. It seemed like the more I showed him and his wife *The Bible Story* set, the more God was working on their hearts. At the close, they just kept going back and forth, asking each other, "What do you think?"

Finally the father looked down at his son and said, "If you read these words, I'll buy the set for you." Little sister was right on the edge of her chair as the little second-grader tried to read *The Bible Story*. As I prayed silently, I could almost sense the angels helping the little fellow read the words aloud. When he finished the paragraph, the father was satisfied. The little boy had read all but one word correctly. The man purchased not only the *Bible Story* set, but also *The Desire of Ages*. As I left that home, I almost felt like crying because God is so good.

Another
Chance

I found out from the post office that the people listed on the lead card were located at the south end of Brunswick, Maryland. When I knocked on the trailer door, I saw that no one was home. I decided to stay in that neighborhood and knock on doors until they came home that evening.

The first family I spoke with wasn't interested. Next I knocked on the door of a big white house. A lady came to the door, and when I told her why I was there, she asked me to step inside. Usually when I meet older people, I show them our religious books instead of the health books because most older people already have health books. I opened my case and brought out *Bible Readings for the Home*, and as I started to tell her about it, her husband asked if we had any other big books. I noticed that something about him was wrong because I could smell liquor on his breath.

I said, "Yes, we have many other religious books."

I brought out some of the other books, but before I ended the canvass, he stopped me short and demanded, "What's the cost of these books?" Then he added, "I know they're good books, but just tell me the cost."

When I told him the cost, he said, "That's enough! We don't need them. Be on your way." It really shook me how this man had cut me short and turned so irritable within just a few minutes.

Then I heard his wife ask him, "Are you going to get the kids from school?"

Reluctantly he told her he would, but looking directly at me, he said, "But don't you be here when I come back."

I started to pack my books back into my briefcase. Just before he went out the door, the man repeated his warning: "Don't you be here when I come back."

His wife told me not to pay attention to him and then said that she liked the book *Bible Readings for the Home*. As we were talking, she happened to mention that her sister had a disease and was a patient at Washington Adventist Hospital. She talked highly of the hospital because it had really helped her sister. When I told her that I was a Seventh-day Adventist, her eyes seemed to glow. She said, "Oh, those beautiful Adventist people!"

Feeling impressed that she would be receptive to the message in that lovely book, I told her, "I know this book will be really beneficial to you and your family."

"I'll take it!" she said. Then she pulled out a $20 bill for the down payment and said she'd like to pay $10 down. I didn't have any change, but she didn't seem concerned. She told me that she'd get change when her husband got home. I thought in the back of my mind, *Yeah, right; I'll bet he'd agree to give me some change!*

We talked for about five minutes more, and then in came the children and the husband right behind them. The look in his eyes could have bored a hole right through me. Just as he got up to me, his wife asked with such a sweet voice, "Honey, do you have change for a twenty?"

He looked at me, and then at her and said, "What for?" She told him about *Bible Readings for the Home* and how it would help them all. To my amazement, he looked at me and said, "Give him the whole thing."

For a minute I thought I would fall off the couch. God is so good. As I was leaving, he said, "Could I ask you one question, young man?"

I said, "Sure, what's that?"

He said, "Do they sell these books in communist countries?"

I said, "I don't think so."

He said, "I wish it was like that here in the United States so men like you couldn't sell these books." I just smiled and walked out, thanking God all the way to my car.

On the road halfway to Frederick, I remembered I had never gone back to visit the people who had sent in the lead card. I pulled the car to the side of the road, trying to decide what to do. Then I said a prayer. "Lord, if there are thirty lead cards in my box, I'll go back."

There were exactly thirty cards in my box.

When I got back to the trailer, the people still weren't home. I knew, though, that God wanted me there for a reason, so I started knocking on some doors. I canvassed one man and found out that his wife had died within the past year. I sold him a *Steps to Christ*.

I was about to leave because I thought this was why God had sent me back. But just as I went around the corner, I saw a certain trailer and pulled over. I went up and knocked on the door, not sure why God wanted me to stop there.

The lady who answered didn't want me to come in, so I started to show her the medical books right there at the door. Finally she let me in. As I went through my presentation, the lady didn't seem interested at all until I got to the seven signs of cancer. Then she said, "Mister, you don't have to tell me about cancer. My mom, my dad, my sister, and my husband all died of cancer. I had cancer of the breast and was the only one who made it."

I showed her what the disease looked like in the pictures, and at the close of the canvass I really prayed hard for Jesus to touch her heart. She took the medical books!

I checked the first trailer one more time, but the people still weren't home so I called it a day. That night when I got home and told my wife about the blessings of the day, I remembered that I hadn't left a religious book with the woman who'd had cancer. I felt really bad about it.

The next day, I went back to Brunswick to call on the people in the trailer, and they were home. They, too, purchased the health books, for which I praised God. But again I left that area without giving the woman with cancer a religious book.

Imagine my joy when, a few days later, as my family and I were in Frederick shopping for groceries, there behind the bakery counter was that same lady! We talked for awhile, and I gave her a *Steps to Christ*. I rejoiced that God had given me another chance to give her one of the books of life.

He Saw My Needs

One day I was traveling down the road, thinking how things weren't going so great. I'd only had a few small sales here and there. But I was praising God for them.

I had a pile of lead cards sent in by people who had seen our display copy of *The Bible Story* books in local doctors' offices, and for some reason I felt like it was going to be a good day for me. It's hard to explain until you have witnessed God's hand in the work.

I knocked on the first door, and the people purchased. The same thing happened at the second door, and at the third, and even at the fourth. As I gave my last canvass that night, God again blessed. It was the biggest day I've ever had.

I left the last home and started up the road. For awhile I didn't say anything. I just thought about how God had blessed me and thanked Him for my little Datsun, which I'd had only one month and which was running so well. I started to sing because I was so happy inside. Then every once in awhile I'd holler out the window, "Amen! Praise God for His beautiful love." As I looked at the cars on the other side of the road, I wondered how many of those people knew Jesus.

Then I heard a bang and a knock in the engine. I didn't know what to do, so I just said, "Take me home, Datsun." Creeping up the side of South Mountain at twenty miles per hour, I barely made it over the top. By this time, the engine was cutting out so badly that I turned the switch off and let the car drift down the other side of the mountain. When we began to level out, I turned the switch on just long enough to get up enough speed to get up to the ramp. Then when I got to the ramp, I turned the switch off and drifted to the stop sign.

The man from whom I'd bought the car lived only two miles away. My house was about six miles away, so I prayed to God that I would make it to Ralph's house.

After a long, slow ordeal I finally pulled into Ralph's driveway. The smoke was rolling out from under the hood as I went up to the door. A young lady answered and said that he was at the prison giving Bible studies. She said Ralph would be home in about two hours and told me she'd call his son, who was giving Bible studies not too far away. About half an hour later Ralph's son pulled in, and we tried to start the Datsun, but it wouldn't start. Finally we gave up and he took me home.

At about 11:30 that night I called Tom Chastang, my district leader, and explained my situation. He said he would be up tomorrow to look it over. Literature evangelists are thankful for district leaders because it seems like every one of them knows something about auto mechanics. We know who to call in a time of trouble!

The next day Tom identified the problem. It was a blown piston in the engine. Tom got his tools, and together we tore that engine apart. Within a week we had the little Datsun running again.

As I look back on that experience, I see that if it wasn't for those five sales and my district leader's ability, my wife and I never could have afforded to fix our Datsun. Now I can see why God blessed me with five beautiful sales that day. God made the profit from what I sold equal the expenses of the necessary repairs. He takes care of His own. "And it shall come to pass, that before they call, I will answer; and while they are yet speaking, I will hear" (Isa. 65:24).

The Customer That Came to Us

While Gary Bevins and I were following up on a lead card, we discovered that the lady who had sent the card in was a Seventh-day Adventist. She was interested in two of our sets for children—*The Bible Story* and *Bedtime Stories*.

After purchasing the books, the lady asked if we would visit some of her friends in the neighborhood. We went a few houses up the road, and the woman who answered the door invited us inside. She visited with us a few minutes and then told us to come back next week.

We were just about to leave when there was a knock at the door. As Gary opened the door to go out, the woman outside stepped right up to him. "Are you the Seventh-day Adventists who are selling those books?" she asked. When Gary replied that we were, she asked us to come to her house next!

We said, "Praise the Lord!"

After we showed her our materials, the lady purchased a year's subscription to both *Life and Health* and *Listen* magazines. We had a very good conversation about Christ, and before we left she had enrolled in a Bible correspondence course. You never know what God has in store from one lead card!

Beyond Belief

I was going from door to door in Westminster, Maryland, when suddenly I heard a voice behind me. I turned around and saw two men putting up a TV antenna. The man on the roof was asking what I was doing. I casually told him I was selling religious books and health books, but I didn't think much about it because I didn't think they were interested. However, the man told me that his wife might be interested in something like that and asked if I could come to his house that night. I took his address and said I'd be there at seven o'clock.

When the time came, I said a prayer and went upstairs. As I spoke with the couple about the books, their interest grew more and more. At the end of the canvass, they purchased the health books, the family Bible, *Bible Readings for the Home*, and a year's subscription to *Life and Health*. I couldn't believe what had happened!

The other man who had been helping to put up the TV antenna had been in the room during this time, and to my surprise, he asked if he could get a set of the health books, too! Although I never would have considered those two men prospects for religious material, God clearly called me to them. We just can't imagine what God has in store for us as we dedicate ourselves to His beautiful work.

The Hitchhiker

In the literature work, you never know who God is going to send you to next. As I was headed down the road toward Emmitsburg, Maryland, I noticed a young man hitchhiking. He looked as though he were limping and in pain. I don't often pick up a hitchhiker, but the Lord impressed me to pick up this young man.

As we were driving down the road, we started talking about religion. The more we talked, the more he wanted to know. When I said I sold religious books, he told me he'd like to look at one of them. As we drove, he read several chapters of *Colporteur Ministry* and said he really enjoyed it.

Finally we came to Emmitsburg, and I stopped to let him off because we were going different ways. Just before we parted, I told him that I had a small book called *Your Bible and You* that has brought many people closer to Christ. After looking at the book a while, he said he would take it. I wrote up the contract and had a word of prayer. Just before he left, he said he would also like to get that *Colporteur Ministry* book.

As I drove on toward Taneytown, I took one more look at the young man who was walking down the road with one of God's books in his hands. Praise the Lord! Even hitchhikers need Jesus.

God's Miracles

I had a lead card from a lady who lived in Frederick, Maryland. But when I introduced myself at the door and showed the card to her, she told me she hadn't sent it in. She said someone must be playing a trick on her.

On the way out to my car, I noticed a man walking across the road. Several moments later I recognized him as someone I'd graduated from high school with, so I decided to follow him back into the alley. I started knocking on doors in the area, but couldn't find him.

At one door, a young man asked me if I sold life insurance. After I explained my work and showed him a few books, he asked if I would go with him to show the volumes to his wife, who was working at Prudential Life Insurance Company.

I agreed, and while there the couple tried to sell me an insurance policy. But I told them that I had something better than life insurance and proceeded to show them the *You and Your Health* medical volumes. One of the life insurance men was Greek, and he agreed with everything in the books. This greatly impressed the young man's wife, and she immediately decided to purchase the books. It just goes to show that God has many ways to work through a lead card. Sometimes when you visit the person listed on the card, it's really because God wanted you to be in that area to witness to the person next door.

The Wrong Door?

I went into a housing development in Hagerstown, Maryland, to ask where a certain lady lived so I could set up Bible studies with her. I couldn't find her house, but I was pretty sure I knew where her cousin lived. So I drove there and knocked on the door, but the lady who answered was not the one I wanted to see. I got the feeling you get when you realize you've gone to the wrong door.

However, I proceeded to tell this lady about our *Bedtime Stories* for children and asked if she would like to see them. She said she would, so I ran back to the car to get my briefcase. As she saw the beautiful books, God impressed this woman's heart, and she bought the set. I had thought it was the wrong door, but God knew it was the right door.

Protecting
Angel

Y ears ago there were problems with the cost of meat prices. They kept going sky high. I was working out in the farmland running leads and cold canvassing. I just went from one farm to the next. I had no idea that people were killing cattle and butchering them right there in the field and taking the meat. They were saying on the radio to be on the lookout for a man with a case. They didn't have any idea what he looked like, but they knew what he was doing.

I did not know anything about this. I came up to this field and the gate was locked, and I just grabbed my case and climbed over the gate where the cattle were. I went up through the field of cows up to the farmhouse.

I walked up to the door and knocked and knocked again, and no one answered. I left a card on the door and started to walk away. About that time the door opened a crack, and the guy asked me what I wanted. I told him what I was doing, and he invited me in.

He kept looking at my case the whole time I was canvassing him. Of course, I had no idea why. I finally opened my case and pulled out *The Desire of Ages*, a beautiful book on the life of Jesus, and showed it to him. The old farmer and his wife really seemed to like that book, and they decided to buy it. After making the sale, I had prayer with them. When I was finished praying and I looked up, there were tears running down the farmer's cheeks.

I was rather surprised, and then he said, "Young man, didn't you know that the cattle were being butchered right in the fields, and they were leaving the carcasses. My neighbor next door lost a number of cattle the other night, and I thought for sure you were that man. When I saw you come up through the field of cows, I put my gun out the window and cocked the trigger. I'm telling you, I pulled and it didn't go off! Somebody spared your life today."

I looked at him kind of shocked and said, "Well, that somebody must have been my protecting angel."

As I left that farm, I realized that many times we have no idea what's going on around us. God had sent His angels that day to protect and spare my life.

Miracle
in the
Laundromat

The address on the lead card read Emmitsburg, Maryland. I found the house quite easily, and when the woman answered the door, she invited me inside.

I had just begun to show her the health volumes when in walked her mom and dad. She then told me that it was her daughter's birthday, and they were about to have a party. I didn't want to hold things up, so I said I'd come back the next week.

When I returned to the house as I had promised, the woman's husband told me that she was down at the laundromat and that she had left word for me to come down there. So I did. I pulled the books out of my big briefcase and showed them to her right there in the laundromat! People were walking all around us and wondering what was going on.

When I walked out that night, she had purchased the health set, a copy of *Bible Readings for the Home*, the family Bible, and a year's subscription to *Life and Health*. Praise the Lord! God uses all places and situations.

Nobody Home

Another day I drove to Sharpsburg, Maryland, to see a family who had sent in a lead card. They weren't home, so I stayed in that area and knocked on other doors in the neighborhood. I went back two or three times that day, but no one was ever home. Late that afternoon I tried one more time, and still the people weren't home.

Then I went to the house directly across the street. They asked if I would come back the next day since they had just sat down to eat supper.

I returned to that area the next day, still hoping to follow up on that lead card, but there still wasn't anyone home. So I went across to visit the people who had asked me to return another time.

The lady at the door said her husband wasn't there yet but that he would be home in a few minutes. He arrived shortly thereafter, and I prayed silently as I told them about *The Bible Story* books. They were really interested, and at the close of the canvass they purchased all of the volumes.

The miracle of this experience is that I never did get to meet the people who had sent in the lead card. God sent me to that area to visit the people across the street.

When God Opens Doors

While visiting one of my former customers at Blue Ridge Summit, I found out that the young man had been laid off and that his wife had left him. He wasn't interested in buying anything more right then.

As I prepared to leave, a little boy from next door said, "Hi, mister!" I didn't think anything about it at the moment, but moments later I thought, *God has given me an invitation.*

The child's mother let me in, but she wasn't interested in what I had to say. The boy's grandmother was, though, and before I was halfway through my canvass, the father came home. He didn't object to my presentation, and the family decided to purchase the Home Library Unit, which consists of our six big books, *The Bible Story* set, and the family Bible.

Afterward, the man told me that he probably wouldn't have let me inside the door if he had been home earlier. I'm so glad God opens the doors!

Six Months
Later

One time my second district leader, Gary Bevins, and I tried to follow up on a lead card that was six months old. The person's home was located up in the mountains around Harper's Ferry, and after a long and futile search, we finally gave up.

On the way back down, we stopped at two houses. At the first, no one was home. Then God impressed me that we should stop at the second place. I told Gary, "I don't know why, but I'm convinced we need to stop at this home." A young lady was working in her yard and invited us in.

I began showing her our beautiful set of *The Bible Story* books, and she became very excited. She said she had been wanting to get an order card from her doctor's office, but the cards were always gone from the books. She happily purchased the set and thanked us for coming to her home.

Before we left, Gary asked the woman if she knew how we could find the house where the lady who had sent in the lead card lived. She told us that it was her sister and that she and her husband were in Florida and would be back in a week. Thanks to God our trip was not in vain!

Where They're Needed Most

I knocked on doors all the way into Leitersburg, Maryland, with no success. However, I was assured that God had something planned for me.

Then I met a Seventh-day Adventist family who told me that the lady across the road bought from every salesman that came around. I went next door to meet her. But when I knocked, the lady's husband came to the door and said they weren't interested. I was one salesman who didn't get in that home! Satan must have been working overtime that day.

I went to the next house and was invited inside. The lady of the house told me that her husband was deceased. She was very interested in the health volumes, and as I told her about them, God touched her heart and she purchased the set. God always leads you to the home where the books are needed most.

The Hiccup

I called on a friend with whom I had graduated from high school and learned that he would not be home until about four o'clock. I decided to visit with some of the people in that neighborhood while I was waiting.

Just before I came up to the first house, I got a very bad case of the hiccups. But I went into the home anyway, praying that God would take them away. But God didn't grant my request, and I hiccuped the whole way through my presentation. Needless to say, I left the home very badly embarrassed.

As the time drew closer for me to go see my friend, I drove around the neighborhood praying earnestly that God would remove those hiccups. Just before four o'clock, I pulled over and prayed one more time. As I ended my prayer, I was impressed by God to eat the cookie left over from my lunch. So I ate the cookie, and before I'd even swallowed it, the hiccups were gone. God performed another miracle for me—not only were the hiccups gone, but my friend purchased the entire Home Library Unit. To God be the glory!

God Didn't
Let It Stop

I was working in Taneytown, Maryland, on a lead card, but the people weren't home, so I decided to knock on doors for awhile. I remembered that just behind where my sister-in-law and her husband lived there was a small trailer court. I drove there and said a short prayer before I got out of my car. Every day, even before I knock on that first door, I always pray for God's angels to be near.

At one of the trailers, a young lady invited me in, and I showed her the *Bedtime Stories*. She purchased that set as well as a copy of *Your Bible and You*. I was so excited as I went to the next trailer!

Next, an older gentleman invited me into his home. As I told him about our health books, I found out that he was dying from cancer. He also told me that he wasn't too fond of salesmen; the last one who had been to his home had actually pulled a knife on him!

The prospects for this man buying any of our books didn't look very good from my point of view, but from God's it was different. He had led me there, and it was up to Him to touch this man's heart.

As I made my presentation, I could sense God and Satan battling back and forth, but I left that home knowing my God had been victorious. The man had purchased the three volumes of *You and Your Health*, *Bible Readings for the Home*, the big family Bible, and a year's subscription to *Life and Health*.

I don't know how some literature evangelists would react after an experience like this, but I was so thrilled that I just couldn't go on in that trailer court. My cup was full to overflowing, but God didn't let it stop there.

Later, when I returned to see how the people were enjoying the books, I was referred to another family interested in the family Bible. They purchased two Bibles— one for themselves and one as a wedding gift for their brother.

Bumper
Sticker

I was working in Delaware and had decided to go back to Georgetown, Maryland. But then, as I went by this one road, the Lord reminded me of a certain trailer court I hadn't visited for about two years. As I drove on, I felt deeply impressed to go to that trailer court. So I turned my car around and drove back.

I went in and started knocking on doors. I had made a few contacts and talked to a few families. Then I decided to leave. I started to pull out, but the Lord impressed me to knock on one more door.

I saw a bumper sticker on the back of this car that said "God loves you." I stopped right there and knocked on that door. A young man came to the door and invited me in. I told him I'd noticed the bumper sticker on the back of his car. He said he did love the Lord but that he hadn't put it there. He'd just bought the car from his neighbor. We had a great discussion, and he was just about to buy the books when the door flew open and in came a lady who was sobbing. He told me that he had to help her and that I'd have to come back another time.

I left feeling discouraged, wondering if Satan had caused the whole scene. But I used the situation as an opportunity to knock on the next door. A woman named Nancy invited me in, and I learned that she loved the Bible books dearly but that her husband believed in evolution.

He'd quit the church three times and didn't believe there was a God. Just a little later, he pulled up into the driveway.

I said, "Nancy, when he comes in and I show him the books if you show that you want them there's a good chance he'll buy them for you and the children. But you have to show that you want them."

Most ladies will not do this; they leave it up to their husbands. But I was hoping and praying that this time would be different and that the Holy Spirit would impress her. As I gave the canvass, Nancy's husband got excited.

I asked, "Will there always be war? Is there a God in heaven that cares?" Then I answered these questions through *The Bible Stories*, pinpointing certain verses. As I closed the sale, the young man was very impressed. His wife said, "Honey, we need these books. Just buy them."

She kept saying that they needed them, and finally he told me to go ahead and write up the contract.

As we were talking for a few minutes afterward, he said, "I'm so glad you came. You've answered many questions I've always wondered about." I had prayer with that beautiful family and then went home.

It wasn't until much later that I found out the lady who had been crying next door was Nancy's mother. She had been living with Nancy two days a week and with her other sons and daughters for a few days each week. But Nancy's husband had gotten tired of it and told her that she couldn't come back. He wasn't a Christian, and he didn't care whether or not Nancy's mother had a place to live.

What is amazing to me is how God led me to a man who didn't believe in God, and by the time I left, the doubt was leaving and belief in God was coming through.

I thank God literature evangelists have the privilege of being His servants, and I pray that every day we go out our precious Lord will go with us to prepare the way.

God Speaks to the Heart

As I was Ingathering, I knocked on the door and told the lady about what I was doing. She gave me a dollar. I happened to tell her I was a Seventh-day Adventist. She seemed like a very nice lady, so I asked her if she would like to know more about our religion, and she said she would.

Months went by and each day I said I would go by and see the lady Satan just kept me too busy with other people and things. Finally one day I went to see them. It was a beautiful visit. Mr. and Mrs. Johnson were really searching. They purchased the medical books and *Bible Readings for the Home*. The greatest blessing was that they asked me to share Bible truths with them. For the next couple of months we studied together every Wednesday night, praying that Jesus would show them new light. They believed everything that was shown them, but then one day they were invited to a Vacation Bible School at a Methodist church.

From that day on, little by little, they talked more and more about the Methodist church. At I stopped by one Wednesday night they told me they didn't want to continue studying anymore for a while because it was just too much at one time.

At least God did show them many new things they never knew before, including the Sabbath. The seed was sown, and we pray the Holy Spirit can reap the harvest.

A Prayer That Was Answered

There was one prayer I always wanted God to answer. Each time I read *Colporteur Ministry*, I was impressed by the statement that, if possible, *The Desire of Ages* should be placed in every home. But for a period of about eight months, I hadn't placed a single copy of *The Desire of Ages* in any of the homes I had visited.

On Monday I really prayed for God to place *The Desire of Ages* in some homes that day. There was one road that I'd always wanted to work but just never had the time until then. This was the day, and I was determined to canvass that road to the end.

I knocked on a few doors and no one was home. About the fifth house an older lady, Mrs. Green, was out in her garden working. I told her what I had to offer and she really wasn't interested. I must have gone through parts of the canvass at least three times, but she just would not respond. We had a beautiful talk about Christ. Just before I was preparing to leave, she asked me again how much *The Desire of Ages* cost. I told her, and she said she would take it. I was so happy I was just bubbling over with joy.

I'll never forget what she said before I left. She said, "If I don't see you here again, young man, I'll see you in heaven." What encouraging words, but that's not all.

I went to the next house, and a young lady purchased a set of our children's books and *Steps to Christ*. After I left her home and went to the next house, the lady invited me in. After talking with her just a little while I found out that she took Mrs. Green to church every Sunday. I explained to her what Mrs. Green purchased, and she purchased *The Desire of Ages* also.

That day my prayer was answered. Isn't it great to be in God's army?

Teamwork

I first met Mr. and Mrs. Larrimore after they mailed in a lead card requesting more information about a book I was selling. Six months after my first visit, I went back to see the Larrimores, and again they purchased several books from me. But then the family moved, and I lost contact with them.

A year later I was going from door-to-door in a certain subdivision when I learned that a Seventh-day Adventist family by the name of Larrimore lived down the street. I immediately went to visit them, and sure enough it was the same family who had purchased our books the year before!

During our happy visit, Mr. Larrimore told me how his family had made their decision to join the Adventist Church. The church members in Grasonville, Maryland, had asked for a list of everyone in that area who had purchased books from literature evangelists. One of those members, Dr. Ralph Libby, had visited each person on the list to invite them to church on Sabbath. It was then that he met the Larrimore family. They had accepted Dr. Libby's offer to begin Bible studies, and later were baptized. This experience reminded me of the text that says, "One sows and another reaps" (John 4:37). What a privilege it is to be part of a team who is working for the salvation of souls!

A Perishing Soul

I had sold a set of books to only one out of thirteen people in a certain apartment house in Braddock Heights, Maryland. So later, I decided to go back and see the other twelve, but most of the people weren't home.

When I knocked on apartment four, I was invited in by a young lady. As I showed her *The Bible Story* books, she said that she had just purchased something like our books from a man who had come just ahead of me. I wasn't sure what to do at first, but then God told me to show her the medical books. I did, and she decided to purchase the set.

Before leaving, I wondered aloud what her husband would say when he came home and found out she'd bought two sets of books that day. She had told me that the man she was living with was not her husband, but that they had three children. But I had invited her to camp meeting and to church and explained a little about our beliefs. And I left her some literature.

When we stray far away from God, our lives can get so mixed up. Yet, isn't it wonderful that God welcomes every searching soul who, as the prodigal son, repents and comes home?

The Big Six

O ne of the happiest days of my life was when six families received the books of life. I was working in Myersville, Maryland, and had made two sales when I ran out of contract pads. I went home to get another one and told my wife that God had already blessed me with two sales.

I'd wanted to stop and see the family just up the road from my house, so I dropped in, and they purchased the medical unit. I immediately went back to my house, got the set of books, and delivered them to the family.

Then I went on down to Smithsburg to see another family who had told me to come back at a later time. This time I canvassed the husband, since he wasn't there the first time. They purchased, as well. When I went back to my house and told my wife the good news, she was as excited as I was.

Next I decided to go to Frederick on a lead card, and by this time it was rather late. The people weren't home, but I remembered that there were two apartments upstairs at the Hillside Motor Inn, which was just down the road. I knew that the family I'd sold to before had moved out and that another family now lived there.

To my surprise, the family who used to live there just happened to be visiting that evening, so they introduced me to the new renters. Halfway through my canvass, the lady who had purchased from me before told her friend how much she had enjoyed the set I was describing. This really helped close the sale for the family that lived there, and they purchased it for themselves. Before leaving, I left them with some free literature.

As I got to the car, I noticed that it was about 9:30 p.m. Usually I don't visit people after 9 o'clock, but I felt impressed to try one more time to locate the family on the lead card. They were home, and after spending forty minutes looking at the health books, they decided to purchase them.

Six sales in one day! As I was going home that night, I simply could not express my gratitude to Jesus. One of the families did cancel their order later on, but I still count it a success because they at least got the free literature I left with them.

Two Sales
Instead of
One

One Friday I took my wife's sewing machine to the Singer shop to be fixed. We decided to purchase a new one for her, and as we were filling out the contract, I was asked to explain my occupation. The sales lady wanted to know what a "literature evangelist" was and exactly what I did for work.

She was very interested in my explanation, and although I didn't have my case with me, it just so happened that I did have a few of our books out in the car.

After seeing what the books looked like, the lady decided to purchase all six of them. As we visited together, we had a wonderful discussion about the Bible.

It struck me as beautiful that while she was writing up our order for something we needed we, too, were able to give her something she needed—the books of life. You never know when or where God will use you to bring a blessing to others.

Nobody Had the Book

O ne day Elaine Furrow called me from the Home Health Education Service. She told me that some members of the Charlestown Church had visited a lady named Mrs. Picket. As they talked, they discovered she was really interested in learning more about the Bible. In Sabbath School one morning, the class decided to buy a copy of *Bible Readings for the Home* for Mrs. Picket. Meanwhile, the Holy Spirit was already at work. He sent me by her home on a lead card for the medical books.

She fell in love with them and also purchased *Bible Readings for the Home*.

When the members of that church found out that Mrs. Pickett had the medical books and a copy of *Bible Readings*, they saw the hand of God at work. They hadn't been able to find the book to give to her—nobody seemed to have one! So God sent a literature evangelist to that home. The Lord knows which of His children want to know more about His precious Word.

Thank God for this great and beautiful work. Thank God that He hears the prayers of His saints and answers them. When they see the miracles He works for and through them, it helps them realize that there is a God in heaven who cares.

Candy Lane

One day during a group canvass, John Creelman and I were working on a street called Candy Lane. We knocked on one door and we could see three children inside eating supper. The oldest brother came to the door and said that his mom and dad were eating out tonight. So I told them we'd try to stop back.

But as we went on, it started to get late, and we decided to leave and go back home. As we went by that house, the Lord impressed me very strongly to stop. I told John we had to make one more call. We went back and knocked on the door. When we told the man who answered what we were doing, he said, "I have to be back to the Chrysler Corporation by eight o'clock, and it's eight minutes till eight right now."

"Sir, just give me a few minutes," I said.

He obliged and invited us in. I showed him *My Bible Friends* very quickly. He told us to wait while he checked with his wife, who was upstairs.

I had told him about the cassettes and how they would be a blessing to his children. He went upstairs, and John and I prayed. When he came back down he told us to go ahead and write up a contract for the books. He bought *My Bible Friends* and the cassettes and *Life and Health* magazine.

This was a beautiful miracle to me. God had impressed me to go back when I forgot about it. In two minutes I showed him the books, and in three minutes I wrote up the contract. It goes to show that if we rely on the Lord, He will bless us because He promised in His Word.

A Wounded Soldier

I was in Frederick, Maryland, when I felt impressed to stop at a certain home. I had talked to the lady who lived there about ten years before, and she had purchased books from me. She had foster children. They were little when I first visited, and now they were all grown up and had married and moved away. She had fostered twenty-five children through the years. We had a good talk, and she bought the medical books.

On my way back to town, I decided to follow up on another lead card. I spotted a telephone booth and pulled up to it. Nobody answered at the phone number on the card, so I headed back to my car. Only then did I notice the little red car parked right beside me.

"Don't I know you?" I asked the guy inside.

He looked at me kind of funny and then said, "You're a literature evangelist, aren't you?" I told him that I was and then gave him my name.

He told me his name was Skip, and then I remembered that he had been a literature evangelist about three years earlier. Sadly, things were falling apart in his life and marriage. His wife was not behind him and didn't want him to sell literature. He told me how his wife would be reading *The Great Controversy* when he came home, but then as he got closer he could see that underneath it she was really reading a romance novel.

He said he had gotten so depressed that he'd used the money he earned from selling books to buy whiskey and beer. He had even thought about committing suicide.

While we talked, Skip sat there with cigarettes in his pocket, a pint of whiskey in

47

one hand, and 7-Up in the other hand. He would drink some whiskey and then some 7-Up. I told Skip that it wasn't a coincidence that we met and that God had arranged this appointment.

This man was really searching, and I took the opportunity to talk to him about God. He already knew what he should be doing, but he was so weak—just like so many of us are. I prayed with him after talking to him. He asked me if I'd come see him, and I assured him I would.

I felt so happy that God sent me to that man who was crying out for help. Our meeting showed me that if it wasn't for this literature work and for a wife who stands behind me and children that support me, I could be like that man.

Fourteen Years

One of the greatest joys in the work is seeing someone from your family come into the message. It took fourteen years for God to work this miracle. I had a cousin about my age named Eddie. His wife's name is Susie, and my wife's name is Sue. He has a boy and a girl, and I have a boy and a girl.

When I first started this literature work, I gave Eddie Bible studies because I sold him and his mom some books. His mom believed most of what we studied except for the Sabbath, the state of the dead, and hell fire. However, Eddie believed. He really truly believed in his heart. He could see it, but he couldn't give up his cigarettes and beer.

Eventually his business transferred him to Frostburg, Maryland. I didn't see him for years.

I got a call one night very late from Charlotte Becker, the teacher who had taught our children when we lived on the Eastern Shore.

She said, "Don, do you know a Charles Draper?"

I said, "No. How many children does he have?"

She said, "He has three girls."

I said, "I know an Eddie Draper, and he has a boy and a girl."

She said, "That's him!"

Come to find out his business transferred him to Baltimore from Frostburg, and he saw this sign about some Revelation meetings being held by Richard Halverson, the evangelist for the conference. He noticed the sign Seventh-day Adventists, and he faithfully came every night. He believed the message, and this time instead of putting it off, he accepted the truth and was baptized. I pray that his wife and children will soon be part of this church. Now there's two of us in the family, and it's so good. It took fourteen years to see Eddie come into this message, but it was worth it.

The
Hand of God
Working

The joy of being a literature evangelist is always planting seeds. I felt impressed to do some cold canvassing when I went to the Eastern Shore for a group canvass, so I went to this brand new little trailer park.

That day I took with me Bill Boyd, the district leader from the Eastern Shore. When we started knocking on doors in that little trailer park, we came across this beautiful older gentleman. We heard a dog barking a little bit, but we heard pretty music. That's why we kept knocking. Finally he came to the door. We told him what we were doing, and he invited us in. At first he hesitated and didn't want to take the time. Bill said some beautiful words at the door that impressed him. Bill asked me to show him the books because Bill was having a problem with his voice that day and wasn't feeling well. I showed him *The Desire of Ages*, the *Triumph of God's Love*, and the other large books. He was really excited about the books. He decided to purchase three of the volumes.

Then he said something very nice. He said, "You know, I heard on the radio that there's a speaker coming to Cambridge, and he's going to be holding some evangelistic meetings on Revelation. But I don't know where it's at or who the speaker is."

We were so excited because we had brochures right in my case for the meetings that Richard Halverson was holding.

We gave him one of the cards. We told him, "The Lord sent us to your home so that you could have this literature." He was really excited now. He could really see the hand of the Lord working. We prayed with him, and he promised us that he'd come to those meetings. You never know what's going to happen when the Holy

Spirit touches a soul. We pray that many will be baptized into the church because of the efforts of loyal, faithful literature evangelists. May God bless us and send us to those precious homes.

The Battle

It's amazing how God can lead. One week it seemed as if the devil was doing everything he could to stop me from putting God's books into homes. Two days out of three I hadn't made a single sale.

On Thursday I got down on my knees and prayed, "Oh Lord, I'm going to be out there to watch You put Your books in the homes." I thanked Him for what He'd given me and went out believing. That morning I didn't sell anything, but I still believed God would work a miracle.

Sure enough, toward evening God opened the windows of heaven, as it says in Malachi 3:10.

I went on a lead card, and the lady bought half a set of *The Bible Story* books. It was a very nice family. Then I went to some apartments in Milford, Delaware. I felt impressed to stop by and see a Christian family, but they weren't home. I knocked on another door and started talking with a young man about health foods. I sold his wife some books and started to leave. But then I noticed a lady pull in who I had tried to sell some books to before, and she had told me to come back. I went over and knocked on her door, and she invited me in. I showed her *The Bible Story* books. She fell in love with them and purchased these beautiful books.

I stopped by to see a family who had purchased two sets of *The Bible Story* books about four months before. The man said, "I want to get the rest of the set."

Then I saw this house and felt impressed to knock on the door. The young lady invited me into her home and told me she was so glad I had come. She had two small children and had been wanting *The Bible Story* books. She even had a card ready to send in. The lady pulled cash out from her purse for the down payment. The Lord indeed opened the storehouse. I had more than $1,000 in sales that day. God is so good! I know that if we just lean on Him and trust in Him He will direct our paths to their homes.

A Touch of Love

Once while working in Cambridge, Maryland, with a group of my fellow literature evangelists, I knocked on the door of a very sweet lady. She said she didn't have any money, but she invited me and my partner inside anyway. She listened with interest as I showed her *He Taught Love* (from *Thoughts from the Mount of Blessings*), a beautiful book that had just come out on the market.

As we talked, she told us that her son was in prison and that she wanted to buy *Lessons Jesus Taught* and *Happiness Digest* for him and some of our paperback *Bedtime Stories* and *The Bible Story* for her grandchildren. We got to share Jesus with this lady for about twenty minutes. It really brought joy to our hearts.

As we were leaving, she gave us a check for about $20 and told us how much she appreciated our prayer for her and for her son. She also wished us Godspeed and hoped we would find many more precious souls in that area that would accept this literature.

It is wonderful to know that people are praying for our success. When God comes, I pray that we shall all unite in the kingdom.

The Face of Jesus

I was working in Georgetown, Delaware, and no matter which way I went on the roads, I just couldn't seem to find this lead. So I stopped at a farm, and an old farmer came out. I asked him if he knew where I could find the address on the card. He didn't, but said I could use his phone to call for directions. I went inside and called the family, who lived about a half mile away.

Then I felt impressed to ask the farmer if he had our books. He said he had *The Bible Story* set for his little four-year-old, so I sat down at the kitchen table to show him and his wife our *Bedtime Stories*. They didn't seem interested. I prayed a little harder and felt impressed to reach into my briefcase and get *The Desire of Ages*. As soon as I'd pulled out that beautiful book, the farmer jumped up out of his chair and exclaimed, "Emma! Emma! That's it, that's it!"

"What's it?" I asked.

He said, "Young man, this morning as I was out in the barn, I turned around and saw this beautiful picture of Jesus' face on the wall. It was the same picture that's on this book! I don't care what it costs; I want that book."

Literature evangelism is God's work, and if you're doing God's work, He will send His angels before you to prepare the hearts of the people. I have seen God go before me time after time to soften and subdue people's hearts.

God Sent You to See Us

One day I got a lead card up in the area of Bridgeville, Delaware. I got directions from the post office, but I still couldn't seem to find the address. I stopped and asked some people. I showed them some of our materials. They were so impressed they bought some of the books for their children.

I went down to the next house and asked them the same question. They didn't know the family. I showed them our books too. They also purchased two of our big, beautiful volumes.

I went to the third house down a dirt lane. I asked them the same question. They did not know these people either, but the lady asked, "What do you have in the case? Let us see what you have." I showed them our books and they were so excited. They purchased our books. The lady said, "Maybe God just sent you to see us. Would you please go see our pastor? He lives down the road about half a mile."

So I did. When I went to see the pastor, he was impressed by the books. The pastor asked me who published them, and then asked me what church I attended. When he found out I was an Adventist, he said, "I understand that Adventists believe that everybody is going to hell, and they are the only ones who are going to heaven."

I tried to share with him that it's not the religion but it's knowing Jesus and that there will be Christians from all religions in the kingdom. He liked what I said. I let him know that Adventists are beautiful people doing a great work.

He purchased *The Bible Story* volumes and *The Desire of Ages*. Before I left I had prayer with this pastor and hugged him. I said, "Now see, Adventists aren't so bad after all." He just smiled and laughed.

Friends, I really believe that God just put me on that road. Maybe I will never find that person. But four precious families bought the books of life. It was a beautiful way that God led. Praise God!

My Friends in Wilmington

Marty lived in Wilmington, Delaware, and I was his district leader. I would drive up and work with him and see his wife, Denise, and their little dog, Peanut. Sometimes I would stay overnight with Marty and Denise and work with some of the other literature evangelists in the area.

Marty and Denise were a great team. Denise worked part time, and Marty worked full time. One time Marty was really sick for a couple of days, and I went up, and Denise and I went out and generated some sales for Marty. Marty had a great singing voice, and I loved to hear him sing. Marty has planted literature in many homes. The time will come when the Lord will reap the harvest from the seeds that were planted.

The Motel

In the area of Pocomoke, Maryland, I ran a lead card from someone who wanted to see *The Desire of Ages*. The name on the card was M.G. White—so close to Ellen G. White, who wrote *The Desire of Ages*.

I pulled in the driveway and knocked on the door, and an elderly lady invited me in to sit down. I started to show her *The Desire of Ages*, and her heart was touched. She loved that beautiful book.

She had quite a story to tell. Some years back she and her husband, who had since passed away, had found a copy of *The Desire of Ages* in a motel room. They had fallen in love with the little book and had purchased a copy for themselves.

She showed me the book, which was very well-marked. Her husband had read it through several times and had kept a record in the front of significant events—either sickness or sorrow—and the page from *The Desire of Ages* that had given him comfort. It was just beautiful how this gentleman had marked the book.

The lady loved *The Desire of Ages,* too, and she purchased a new copy for herself. It was interesting sitting there talking to Mrs. Margaret White. I prayed with her and told her that if I never saw her again here on this earth, I would see her in the kingdom. When I finished praying, she had tears in her eyes because I had prayed that the Holy Spirit would impress her through that book and help her to become stronger.

As we go out from door to door, God has ways and means to witness to these beautiful people. And when we take care of their needs, He supplies our needs. Thank God for a wonderful Savior!

The Baptism

The miracles God performs brings the greatest joy to a literature evangelist. In March of 1988, we had a group canvass in Cambridge, Maryland, and God really worked some miracles. A pastor named George from the Rock Hall Church came and worked with us that day—just one day. He had paid accounts that he also wanted to run in his area. So they put George with me for the day, and we really prayed that God would work miracles.

Well, God surely did bless us. We went to a paid customer, a lady living in Trappe. She wasn't home, so we went on to Easton. We came back that night and called on her again. Her name was Mary Johns. She was a sweet young lady in her 30s. She invited us in and said, "You're back again, Don? I don't have any money yet." She had purchased two books from me.

As I talked with Mary, I noticed some Voice of Prophecy lessons on the table. She said she was having difficulty understanding the one she was working on, so I offered to help. George came over, and together we went through the first study. Then I asked Mary, "Did you ever take Amazing Facts lessons?"

She said, "Yes! And I was baptized." George and I looked at each other, and then I asked, "You were? Where?"

"I was baptized into the Seventh-day Adventist Church in Grasonville," she replied. Then she said that after her baptism, her sister also was baptized the year before during Richard Halverson's meetings in Grasonville.

We were really excited. We didn't know what to say. We had asked for a miracle that day, and God showed us a miracle. What a joy it is, my friends, to know that these kind of things happen. If we wouldn't have gone to visit our paid-in-full customers, I never would have known that Mary Johns and her sister were baptized. Many times literature evangelists never know which precious souls have been won to Jesus through their efforts. What a joyous reunion it will be when we get to heaven!

But I thank God that I had the joy of knowing here and now that this young lady and her sister were baptized into our church. Now Mary is giving Bible studies to a lady she knows, and soon she too may be baptized into the church. Continue to pray for this great work and for the coming of our Lord.

Miracles
Never Cease

I n the beginning of this book I related a story about Mike and Sue Johnson. Many years ago I sold them books, and Mike and his family came into the Seventh-day Adventist Church as a result.

I hadn't seen Mike and Susie for almost ten years. Then something very precious happened after I moved back to western Maryland after working for nine years on the Eastern Shore. One Sabbath at the Willow Brook Church, a young man walked up to me and said, "Are you Don Draper?"

"Yes, I am," I replied.

He said, "You probably don't remember me, but I'm Mike Johnson. I was baptized many years ago in the Thurmont Church."

Then I remembered the story of how God had worked a miracle in the lives of him and his family. It was beautiful timing for this reunion, because Mike told me that about a month before his three children had also been baptized into the Seventh-day Adventist Church. Knowing that all through these years they had remained faithful and that their children were being raised in the church made me feel so good.

Then Mike told me another beautiful story. He said that through his ministry he'd won a husband, wife, and their three children into the message and that the entire family had been baptized into the church. So there were eight precious souls redeemed as a result of my Bible studies with Mike and Sue. It shows how God works through the years. Though we move on, the literature program continues to work through the Holy Spirit.

At the time of our reunion there at the Willow Brook Church, Mike was working at the Review and Herald Publishing Association, which prints the books I sell. It made me feel good to know that I was selling the books—God's books—made at the Review, and that Mike was playing a part in the ministry by keeping the Review running smoothly.

My friends, if we stay close to Jesus, who knows how many precious souls we'll see in the kingdom.

Christian Teacher in a Public School

As I was advertising one day in Salisbury, Maryland, I met a lady in the doctor's office. She told me she had *The Bible Story* books. She asked me to stop by and show her the *Bedtime Stories*. A few nights later I stopped, but she wasn't home.

A few houses down the street there was Christian music playing. I stopped and showed our beautiful material. The people were so excited. They bought our books. I had prayer with this family. They said, "Thank God that He sent you today to see us."

I told them how God led me through the music they were playing.

Well, a few days later I stopped by again to the original house I had stopped to visit, and the lady was home and invited me in. I started to show her our material. She was a school teacher in Salisbury. She was a very nice lady.

She told me how she was trying to work with some of the children in the school there who had problems. One boy especially, a blond-haired boy, came from a broken home, and his daddy abused him. He just felt so down all the time. She had prayer with these children in school. She tried to teach them a little bit about Christ. She was going to buy the *Bedtime Stories* and put them in the school and read them to the children every day. I thought that was great.

But the story she told me really touched my heart. She told me how this little boy had missed school for a couple of days and how, when he came back, he'd brought a revolver with him. He got a few of the teachers in the office and said he was going to kill each one of them. They called the sheriff, and this woman noticed the patrol car when she walked by the office. She wondered why the sheriff was there.

She decided to go into the office to see what was going on, and just then the little boy with the revolver saw her out of the corner of his eye. His heart melted, and he dropped the revolver. What an influence that Christian teacher had over the little boy! He told the sheriff later that he had planned to kill all nine people. There were nine bullets in the revolver.

Praise God for Christians in public schools who are willing to share Christ! And thank God for sending me to that home so these books could get into that school

Tears of Joy

We had a group canvass at Salisbury, Maryland, in August of 1988. The Lord really blessed us there. We had lead cards for all over the area in Delaware and Maryland. Paul Hutchins was working down in the Pocomoke area, so they gave me the lead cards Paul had. Working by twos that day, we went down to Eden, Maryland. We ran this lead card, and it was in a little trailer park.

The day before I had told Paul that he ought to try a little trailer park down there close to Eden because the Lord had really blessed me in that trailer park. Now the Lord sent me with these two leads right back to that trailer park.

We knocked on the door and an older gentleman invited us in. Soon we found out that the family members were former Adventists. They had drifted out of the church and went back to smoking. The husband had been able to quit for a while, but the wife was still at it. We had the joy of sharing Christ with this family. We prayed and talked seriously with them, but in a loving manner.

They purchased the medical books and six of the big volumes. But the most beautiful thing is that when I finished praying, this gentleman was crying. Tears were rolling down his face. This really touched us, because it reminded us that so many people are searching. This man just wanted somebody to care about him.

I told him the local pastor would be coming by to see him. The pastor, of course, said he'd go to visit him. The timing was perfect because Tom Hughes was just beginning evangelistic meetings there. We prayed for a good harvest.

Publishing Director

Some of my greatest days have been those on which my publishing director came to work with me. To my joy, Jerry Fletcher moved into the area. He had only been in the position three or four months when he called and said, "I'd like to work with you on Thursday, Don." I was really excited because I knew God would bless us.

We headed to Hancock, Maryland, where I had an appointment that morning on a lead card. I had tried to catch the lady the day before, but she wasn't home. When we arrived, she invited us in. She thought we were selling World Book Encyclopedias, and we told her that we had something much better.

We showed her *The Bible Story* set and the *Bedtime Stories*. She really liked the books and bought the first five from *The Bible Story* set and the *Bedtime Stories* with *The Desire of Ages*. She said she would get the rest of *The Bible Story* books in four or five months.

We asked her if she knew anybody else who would like these books of life. She told us she had a friend who worked at the video store in Hancock who might enjoy these books for her children. We had prayer for this lady and then left to visit her friend, Pam.

Jerry showed Pam the books and I prayed. God opened her heart, and she bought all the same books her friend had purchased. This lady was a Christian, and people were coming in and out of the store as we showed her the books. We had prayer with Pam and could see the Holy Spirit really working. We were so glad her friend had told us about going to see her.

We went back to Hagerstown on another appointment I had as a referral. This family bought the *Bedtime Stories* for their children.

When we looked back over the day, Jerry and I could see how the mighty hand of God had moved. We had more than $700 in sales and almost $400 as add-on contracts. It's always nice when the publishing director can work with us and together we can see the mighty hand of God moving upon hearts.

Looking for the Light

When I moved back to Western Maryland, Chris Simons gave me his leftover lead cards for that area. He and his family were moving on to Ohio, where he would work as a district leader.

One card he gave me was about three or four months old. It was torn and wrinkled with fingerprints all over it. It looked as if the kind of lead you almost have to throw away. But I could still read the address, so I went by the home. After several unsuccessful attempts to find the person home, I decided to enroll him in the Amazing Facts Bible course. I always enroll every lead in Amazing Facts.

Finally, I decided to try one more time. I felt impressed by the Lord to go back. I prayed, "Lord, this will be the last time I go to this house."

Sure enough, this time the man was home. Jerry invited me into his home, and I could see that he was a very nice fellow. I started to show him *The Bible Story* volumes he had asked to see, but I found he was more interested in the Conflict of the Ages series. As I went through the canvass, I found out that Jerry had two sons, one nineteen years old and one fifteen.

Toward the end of the canvass, Jerry said, "You know, the reason why I want these books is because I've found so much light in the Bible recently."

"What do you mean?" I asked.

He said, "Well, did you know that Sabbath is not Sunday, but Saturday?"

I said, "Where did you get that?"

He said, "It's in the Bible—all through the Bible, even the Ten Commandments."

I sat back and asked Jerry a few questions, and he showed me some Scripture. It was enjoyable to see how much this man knew about the Bible.

Jerry was in his middle 40s. He bought the eight big books, six big volumes, plus *Daniel and the Revelation*. I asked him where he had picked up the lead card.

He said, "Well, I did Bible studies through the mail with the Voice of Prophecy. When I finished all of the lessons, they sent me this little card. They thought I might be interested in more literature. I sent the card in months ago."

I told him how both Chris Simons and I had tried several times to catch him but could never find him home. Then I told him how I had almost given up on him and then decided to try one more time.

After my visit with Jerry I sent Adam Stramel, a Bible worker, to see him. They started studying the Bible together, and Jerry went to church with me every Sabbath. After months of studies, Jerry was baptized and is now an elder in the church.

God is working in mysterious ways. Many times the card we think might not be a good card is really the best card of the bunch. We must pray that God will guide us to these homes and that the people will be home. Then we can watch God work the miracles.

God Will Lead

O ne of my prayers is that God will always lead me to those who are really praying for miracles and who want our books of life. One day I had been trying to catch a lady who was a former Adventist.

The interesting thing about Carol is she and her sister were brought into our message from a tract I left in her door.

I never gave her a Bible study. She sent in the tract for Amazing Facts, took the studies, and was baptized into the Thurmont Church. She witnessed to her friends and parents and they, too, were baptized. Unfortunately, she was kind of backslidden out of the church. Her dad had died, and she was discouraged over some problems in the church.

I got to share with her and her husband our books and our message and tried to encourage them to go to the church in Frederick where they were living. Her husband was not an Adventist, but he was open and wanted to know more. We went over to Amazing Facts and talked with a young couple there who said they would give them Bible studies.

It's just so wonderful to know we're working as a team. As literature evangelists, we planted the seed, then Amazing Facts started to reap it, and when the minister baptized them the harvest was done. We can't finish this alone. The literature evangelist needs the laypersons and the ministers behind him or her. By working together we can finish this work and go home. That is my greatest desire.

My Family's Prayer

W hile going door to door on the Eastern Shore of Maryland, I was invited into the home of a very nice family. As I was visiting with them and showing them our books, they seemed to like the books but just wouldn't make a commitment. I tried three or four times to show the wife why she needed these books in her home, and then finally gave up.

Just then, the woman looked at her husband and said, "Let's get these books." It was clear that God had miraculously touched their hearts.

Back at home that night, I was telling my wife and children how that family just wouldn't make a decision and then suddenly changed their minds. Sue asked me what time of day it had been when the woman had changed her mind.

"It was about 3:30 p.m.," I said. Sue looked at the kids, and they looked at her. Then she told me that just before 3:30 that afternoon she had felt impressed to call the kids in from playing to have prayer for their daddy.

Now I could see the full miracle. God had used my family to help close that sale. Thank God for families who are behind us in this great work God has called us to do!

Five Years Later

At a rally at the church in Dover, Delaware, a lady got up and told how the Holy Spirit had worked in her life. Five years before a literature evangelist had come to her door and sold her and her daughter some books. After reading the books, she started studying the Bible and had just that year been baptized into the Seventh-day Adventist Church in Dover.

What joy it was to listen to this woman and to know that the Holy Spirit had used me to touch her life. The literature evangelist plants this beautiful seed and goes on his or her way. Then, years later, God reaps the harvest, and that's how this mother and daughter joined our church. Praise God for these precious souls.

We Pray;
God Hears

Y ou know, when we pray, God hears those prayers, and He will answer them. One day I was running a lead card close to Westminster, Maryland. This was a few years back, but it was such a beautiful experience. As I was running this lead card, I went by a trailer, and the Lord impressed me to stop there.

I said, "Lord, I'll stop on the way back. I'd like to try to catch this lead card."

So I went on with the lead card, and I had a visit with the lady, showed her the books, and sold some small literature.

On the way back, I forgot about that trailer. But God didn't. As I went by, God said, "Whoa, Don!"—just like that! I stopped the car, looked around, and there was the trailer.

I said, "Lord, I'm sorry. Thank you for reminding me."

You know, it's beautiful to know that God talks to you in your mind. You know He loves you. I tell the Lord every day that I love Him, and He tells me right back. I know it's God talking; I know His voice.

I backed up and pulled in the driveway. The lady was out hanging up clothes, and I started talking to her. I told her what I was doing, and she started laughing. I wondered what I'd done wrong. Then she told me her story. She pulled a little card out of her purse. She said, "I just picked it up to send in."

It was precious. She was laughing, and I was laughing. I said, "Well, maybe if you'd sent that card in, nobody would have come. Maybe that's why God impressed me to stop now."

She bought the books, and we prayed together. As I was pulling out of her driveway, it occurred to me what might have happened if God hadn't have told me to stop. Or what if I wasn't in communication with God? May God help us as literature evangelists, laypeople, and ministers—whoever we are, whatever work we do—to keep our hearts open so that the voice of God can speak through us.

The Young Pastor

This is a beautiful story that happened up in Hancock, Maryland. I went to see Ricky Ray who I'd sold books to before. Ricky was really excited to see me because he wanted the rest of *The Bible Story* books for Christmas.

He asked me, "Don, would you go to see my pastor? He just moved in the area. He's a young minister and has two little children. I think he'd really like to see your books because he's been borrowing my books and just loves them."

I drove up to see the young pastor and had a wonderful visit with him and his wife. They wanted to get the books, but at that time they just couldn't afford them. They prayed about it and said that if the Lord willed it, they would get the books as soon as they were able.

We left it in the Lord's hands, and after I left I didn't think about it anymore. A couple of months later, I was in that area again and the Lord brought the young minister to my attention. I stopped by to see him, but he wasn't home. As I was leaving I saw him coming in with another pastor, so I decided to come back later.

I returned a few hours later, and he and his wife and children were home. I sat down and talked to them. They told me they had been trying to reach me. He had called Rick to get my phone number because they wanted to buy those books. I told them that God knew they wanted those books and how He had impressed me to go to Hancock that day.

I was writing up the contract and the pastor told me how they had gotten a check from his grandparents for the little ones to put into savings for Christmas. He told them that instead of putting it in savings, he'd rather buy *The Bible Story* books. The down payment was almost the exact amount he had gotten for Christmas. They bought *The Bible Story* set and *Bedtime Stories* because he wants to share the stories with the young people.

The seed has been planted, and the Holy Spirit will reap the harvest. Someday many people, like this young pastor and his wife, will be a part of the remnant church. I want to be a part of finishing this work.

The
Call Back

We were in a trailer park near Fruitland, Maryland, and I felt impressed to stop at a home where I had sold books several years ago.

Barbara invited us in. She had attended evangelistic meetings years ago. She liked what she had heard but never was baptized.

Barbara was really depressed and had so very many problems. She was trying to get off welfare by working. Then they gave her a raise, and the welfare dropped her food stamps. She only got a quarter-an-hour raise, and she had gotten $25 worth of food stamps. They told her to just go back on welfare, but she didn't want to. She wanted to work.

She told us how different things were breaking down. She reached over to turn the air conditioner on, and it wouldn't start. It would start for a little and cut right off. She tried it four times and every time it cut off. We bowed our heads and prayed that God would work a miracle. After we prayed I said, "Now you go out and turn that air conditioner on, and we'll see what God can do."

She turned the air conditioner on, and it started right up. We were there for another twenty minutes, and the air conditioner ran perfectly. That lady was so happy she'd seen God work a miracle right there. She cried when we prayed with her.

She didn't buy anything; she already had many of our books. God sent us back to that lady because she was discouraged. I thank God that He sends us to individuals like that. Many times we don't know, but our heavenly Father does. Praise God!

The Holy Spirit Impressed

I t was really cold one day I was knocking on doors down in Middletown, Maryland, so I decided to go work in an apartment complex. Hardly anybody was home, but I felt impressed that God had someone there He wanted me to see. At the very last apartment, a young man opened the door. As soon as I told him what I was doing, he invited me inside.

I had barely begun to show the young man and his wife our books when he said, "I might as well go get my checkbook because I already know that we want these books. We were just discussing this."

I sat down and showed them our books, and they just loved them. It was probably the easiest presentation I had ever made because their minds were already made up when I started. I marveled as this beautiful young couple bought *My Bible Friends*, *The Desire of Ages*, and the Bible cassettes for their little girl. Before I left the apartment, we all had prayer together.

It was clear the Holy Spirit had touched their hearts before I ever knocked on their door. God had set up that appointment, and He impressed me to find their door. If we stay close to Jesus, we'll see many more experiences like this in the days ahead.

A Lady's Prayer

A lady in Georgetown, Delaware, was praying for me to come back so she could buy the *My Bible Friends* tapes for her children and her church.

That same morning I woke up and felt impressed to go to Georgetown. I didn't know why, and I kept thinking that it didn't make sense to go to Georgetown. I didn't have any lead cards there but had plenty for Salisbury, Maryland. The more I thought about it, the more I felt impressed.

I went to Georgetown but had no idea where I was supposed to go. I kept thinking, *Lord, is this the street you want me to take?* Some people would have thought I was losing my mind, but I know when God talks. He tells all literature evangelists where He wants them to go.

After driving down practically every street, I finally felt impressed to stop at a house on a back street. I had never been there, but I walked up and knocked on the door. The lady opened the door and said, "Don Draper! I just want to ask you one question. Did they make the cassettes for the *My Bible Friends* books I bought some time ago?"

Suddenly the lady began to look familiar, and I told her that yes we did have the cassette tapes available.

She said, "Thank you, God!" Then I realized why I went to Georgetown, Delaware. God used me to answer this lady's prayer.

A Mother's Prayer

O n my wife's and my twenty-first wedding anniversary, we went back to visit the little church on the Eastern Shore where we had been members for nine years.

We decided to go to Ocean City and stay all day Friday, then get a motel nearby and go to our little church the next day to see the ones we loved so dearly.

The pastor had just had a slight heart attack and couldn't be there, so I had the joy of teaching the Sabbath School, and his wife read the sermon. It was so good to visit with those beautiful members again.

During Sabbath School one of the members mentioned that a young man who had taken Bible studies from me and my wife had been baptized a month ago into that church.

I was so excited. I was hoping and praying I'd see him. Sure enough, when church started, I looked back and there sat Jeff Christopher and his bride-to-be. After church I got to shake his hand and hug him. He told me he was getting married in September and that it would be an outdoor wedding. He showed me the Bible I had given him one night when he called me up and asked me if I'd get him a Bible. It was just beautiful to know that he was a part of our message.

See, my friends, we move on but the written word remains. Jeff's mom is an Adventist and had prayed for him for many, many years. Jeff had grown up with God's books in the home, but it just took him a few years to take his stand for Christ. Praise God that Jeff is a part of His family! May God give him strength to endure as a soldier of God to the end.

Send Me a Christian, God

I was getting ready to go home after working a long day near Hagerstown, Maryland. As I pulled up to a light, there were a couple of cars pulled up behind this one vehicle. As the vehicles kept going around it, I noticed a young lady was standing beside the car, her head bowed down. I had to go around her because vehicles were behind me, and the light was green. I went across the road and pulled over. The light kept changing, and nobody stopped to help the lady. I could tell she was upset and needed help. She didn't know what to do with her car.

I turned around and went back. Before I went up to her, I prayed that God would give me the right words to say.

I asked her if she could use some help. She said her car just would not start. I told her to get inside the car, and I would give her a push by hand. There was a school right beside the light, so we pushed it down there into the parking lot. I asked her if I could help by taking her to a phone or to her house.

She said, "Yes, I'd be glad if you could take me home."

Once inside my car, the young lady said, "You know, I wouldn't get in just any car."

"What do you mean?" I asked.

She explained, "I'm a Christian, and I prayed that God would send a Christian to help me. When I saw your car pull up, and I saw *The Bible Story* sign on the side, I wasn't afraid anymore because I knew you were a Christian."

My friends, we can be a witness wherever we go. When we ask the Lord to lead us, He never lets us down. I gave the young lady a little *Happiness Digest*. God truly blessed.

I Beat the Card!

As I was on my way to Salisbury, Maryland, I remembered a trailer park in Laurel, Delaware, that I had worked in. It was a beautiful day; the sun was shining and it was warm. I just started knocking on trailers, going from door to door.

I was mostly selling small literature and praying that I could put some larger books in some homes.

As I was leaving, I noticed a car pull in the driveway of a trailer where there was many children's toys. I felt impressed to stop when I saw the lady get out of her car with her little girl and go in the trailer. But I thought I'd catch her another time, so I left.

But as I was driving down the road, I felt so impressed to go back to see that lady. Again I could hear God talking to me. I went back to the trailer and knocked on the door.

The lady invited me in, and I started to show her the books. She started to smile and just kept smiling at me. I was getting rather uneasy like something was wrong with me.

She said, "My little girl and I just came from the doctor's office. We were looking at your books while we were there. We pulled out a card from the book and stopped at the post office to mail it."

I said, "Well, I beat the card!" Then we both laughed. I explained to her that sometimes when people send in a card, it doesn't always get to its destination. Maybe God knew that her card would get lost so He sent me "special delivery" right to her home.

She bought the books, and we had prayer. As I was leaving that home, I really thanked God for impressing me to go back to see this lady.

The Dumpster

I had just visited a family near Chambersburg, Pennsylvania, when I passed by a nice new home that was being built. I felt impressed to go back to it, so I turned around and went up and knocked on the door. A young lady answered, so I pulled out my briefcase and showed her a page from *The Bible Story* set. She smiled at me and said, "I have an interesting story to tell you."

Then she explained that when she and her sister were little girls they had loved to go to the doctor's office in order to look at and read those beautiful *Bible Story* books. "Before long," she said, "we both started going to the chiropractor every other Friday. We loved it because that way we could read your books several times each month!"

After she had grown up and gotten married, she looked out her window one day and saw a lady throw a big box into the neighborhood dumpster. "I got curious," she confided, "so after she left I went down and looked in the dumpster. Down at the bottom I saw your beautiful *Bible Story* books. I looked around to make sure nobody was watching and then started putting all of the books back into the box. For some reason the lady had torn out some pages in the first three books, but I gathered them together and put them in the box, as well.

"I bruised my knees up pretty bad in that dumpster," she said. "But then I crawled out and was so happy as I got back to the house and looked through those books I'd always enjoyed as a little girl!"

God works in marvelous ways. That lady told me she still had those patched-together books she'd rescued from the dumpster. She also asked me to come back in a few weeks so she could buy some more of our beautiful books. I pray that more people will cherish our books as much as this woman did.

Planting
Seeds for Us

I got this lead from the Chambersburg Fair, and I went into Pensylvania and ran into this lady upstairs whose name is Judy. It's a beautiful story. You see, Judy is not an Adventist. I looked on her bookshelf as I was talking with her when she invited me in her home, and she had almost all of our books on her shelves. So as I talked with Judy, I found out that she worked at the hospital in Chambersburg and that she loved to pass out literature. She asked me if I had any small literature she could purchase and hand out in the hospital as a witness. I thought, *What a great way to witness!* She bought *Steps to Christ, God's Answers to Your Questions,* and several copies of *The Great Controversy.*

Each time we come out with new material, I go back to see Judy, and she buys more books. One year at Christmas time, she bought about ten small paperback Magabooks, the *Bedtime Stories* set, and *The Bible Story* to hand out at the hospital to her friends who had children. What a way to witness! She would sometimes spend $40-$50 on a case of *God's Answers* to hand out free to patients. Judy doesn't realize it, but she is planting God's seeds for us. I wish we had a thousand people out there like Judy! One year at camp meeting, I bought a bunch of books and took them up to her. She bought them and handed them out.

One time a lady called me up and said she had a bunch of small books in her house and wondered if I knew anyone who could pass them out. I went over there and picked them up, and it was a bunch of small books about marriage and divorce and how to train small children. So I took them to Judy, and she took them and handed them out to her friends at the hospital. She is a living testimony of what we all should be like. God help us all to be like Judy so we all can work together and soon go home to see our wonderful Savior.

A Living Testimony

This story is about another young lady named Judy. I got this lead card and went up to see her. And as I was visiting with Judy, I learned that she wasn't quite seventeen years old. She was still in high school and was working part time at Walmart in Shippensburg and wanted to buy *The Bible Story* books for her brother and sister for Christmas. I showed her the books, and she was all excited about them. Her dad said he'd co-sign for her.

I thought, *What a beautiful testimony! Here's a girl, just 16 years old, buying these books for her brother and sister so they could learn about Christ. The whole family will benefit from this.*

This young girl, instead of buying the things she wanted, purchased about $400 worth of Bible books because she wanted her brother and sister to know more about Christ. She's a living testimony of what a Christian should be like. And when this world ends, I pray that this young lady and her mother and father and sister and brother will be in the kingdom.

Like I have said before, many of these people may never come into our church. But as they read these books, they'll find new light, and they'll live up to the light God gives them. And God will give them the light they need to carry them through to the end. I thank God that I have the joy of meeting people like this every day and seeing those beautiful miracles come to fruition. Thank you, Jesus, for young ladies such as Judy.

Don't Bypass Anyone

I was running leads in Mercersburg, Pennsylvania, and I was heading up to the mountains in McConnelsburg to see a young family I'd sold books to. As I went by this one farm, I felt impressed to stop, but I thought, "Well, I'll stop on the way back."

On the way back, I felt impressed to stop, but I had a lot of leads to visit, and I was tempted to pass by again. But as soon as I passed by the house, I immediately knew I'd done the wrong thing, so I pulled over to the side of the road, turned around, pulled into their nice, long driveway, and went back to that farmhouse.

When I got out of the car and walked around the corner, I saw this great big dog lying in the yard sleeping. I thought, *If I go up to this house and knock on the door and nobody's home, this dog might tear me up! And even if the people are home, if he's a mean dog, he might get to me before they get to him!*

I've been bitten a couple of times by dogs, and it wasn't any fun. So I was determined that this time, I wasn't going to get bit!

I had decided I would just leave some literature on the people's car and hoped that maybe God could use that to impress the people. But then I heard somebody on the back porch, so I peeked around the corner of the house. A young man in his mid-30s was on the porch with his son, and he told me to come on around to the back.

Well, sure enough, as I walked back, the dog started coming toward me. But, thankfully, the man on the porch called to the dog, and it left me alone. I walked up to this young man, introduced myself, and showed him some of my books. He just smiled at me and said, "You'll never believe this, but my wife and I just came from our doctor's office, and we saw *The Bible Story* books there. We thought they would be something really nice for the kids, so we took the card and were just about to mail it in!"

Then the man invited me inside to meet his wife, and we sat around the table talking for awhile. They had just come out of the Catholic church and were now attending a Lutheran church. They told me how they'd found Christ and how excited they were that they could talk straight to God and that they didn't have to go to confession anymore. They were simply thrilled about their new religion.

As we talked I also learned that the young man had fallen off a ladder at work and broken his back. Even though they were living off workman's compensation and didn't have much money, they said they wanted to see all the books I had.

He said, "In a few weeks, if my back heals all right, I'll be going back to work, and when I do I'd like to get some of these books for my children." He had two children. I showed him some of the paperback books and other inexpensive sets, and they went ahead and bought those books. I pray that when they read these books, God will show them more light, because that's what it's all about.

I thank God that He made me go back to that house so I could visit that young man and his wife and two children. Just think—I might have missed out on the joy of seeing them in heaven throughout eternity.

When God impresses us, we must not turn and walk away. On the job or wherever we are, we need to share Jesus. People are crying out for help, and we need to share our Savior. After all, if someone hadn't taken the time to share Jesus with us, we wouldn't be in this great church today

Through the years, I've made so many friends as a result of visiting with people in their homes. I think of Bob and Deborah Brittingham, who have purchased books from me so many times. And because of their testimony, Deborah's mom and her two sisters have also purchased the books of life.

I thank God every day that He has called me to go where ministers and laypeople don't always go—into the homes of God's children. Many have told me that they've never had anybody pray with them in their home. I've seen grown men cry and young ladies weep over the fact that someone cared enough about them to pray with them in their home. I've also seen the expression of joy on children's faces when they know that Mommy and Daddy have decided to buy them these wonderful books.

The Pastor

When I moved to the Eastern Shore of Maryland, I met a very special pastor, Ken Cartwright. He was a great man of God. He had three boys who were about the age of my son, Michael, and daughter, Danielle, at that time. For nine years when I lived on the Eastern Shore, I had many great times with Ken. He was the kind of pastor who you could turn to with any problem.

Ken Cartwright did something I've never seen before. Whenever I had a sale, Ken would want to go see the people. So Ken followed up with Bible studies with the people I sold books to for about seven years. We had more than forty some baptisms from Ken studying with the families after I sold them books. God used this minister in a tremendous way.

Sometimes the pastors that work with you have canvassed themselves, like the pastor I'm working with now, Chris Holland, and have enjoyed it. They said it has helped them to become a better pastor. I thank God for pastors and laypeople who work together as a team.

The Loss of a Friend

F rank was a very good friend who was in the literature work. He would call me and talk to me on the phone. He worked in Ohio, and I worked in Pennsylvania. Well, one day Frank told me he had hit the Promised Land.

A lady had sent a card in, and Frank went to see her. This lady was interested in putting books into the homes of her loved ones and also in some of the churches she visited. So when Frank went back a couple days later after he prayed about it, she purchased twenty sets of *The Bible Story*, ten sets of the *Bedtime Stories*, ten sets of *My Bible Friends*, four of the large books and many paperback books.

Frank said, "Don that was the biggest sale I ever had." He was so excited. He asked me to please pray that this lady wouldn't cancel this order. A couple of days went by, and she didn't cancel and all those books were placed in many different homes and churches.

It just goes to show you that as we get closer and closer to the end of time, the Holy Spirit is being poured out and touching hearts to place seed as fast as possible into homes and churches. God is great

Years later, Tony Mecozzi, another literature evangelist friend, called to tell me that Frank had passed away. Won't it be wonderful to see each other in heaven and talk as we did that day.

The Lady
Next Door

As I was cold canvassing one day in Chambersburg, Pennsylvania, I knocked on the door, and a lady answered it and invited me in. I sat down and was showing her the *Bible Stories,* and she really liked the books and decided to buy some from me.

A little boy was sitting there, and he looked over at me and said, "Mister, today's my birthday."

I said, "Really! How old are you?"

He said, "I'm twelve years old."

It was really great because this little boy wanted the books so badly, and his mom bought the books for him for his birthday. Then he said as I was walking to the door, "Mister, you're a nice man." That made me feel so good!

As I went out to get in my car, I looked over and saw toys at this one house across the street. I went up and knocked on the door. A lady came to the door, and I told her what I was doing. She invited me in, and as we sat down, she said, "You can tell me anything you want, but don't talk to me about religion."

I thought, *Oh boy*. So I prayed, and the Holy Spirit impressed me to show her the Uncle Arthur *Bedtime Stories*. I opened the book and told some stories to her. She didn't say anything, so I got a little bold and I said, "Well, you know sometimes we lose loved ones in this life or we go through hard times."

A little girl ran by, so I started showing her the *Bible Friends*. As I was just getting finished, the lady stopped me and said, "You know, years ago, I lost my sister. She was around twenty years old. I prayed that God would not take her and that she wouldn't die. But she died, and I was so upset. About a year later, my little two-year-old daughter got sick. I prayed again that God would not let her die, but my child died. I walked away from the church and haven't been back since. Then you knocked at my door. It's really interesting because this week, I've been thinking about church, and now you've come to my home. I feel that God sent you."

She didn't buy much from me, but I gave her books. I had prayer with her, and she cried and thanked me again and again for coming.

People are out there hurting. They don't know what you know. If we sincerely pray, God will send us to those people because time is short. I'm so thankful that I listened to the Holy Spirit and went next door because next door was a wonderful family in need of a Savior.

I Need These Books

I had a lead from Emmitsburg, Maryland. A young lady named Ginger sent the card in, and I went by a couple times on my way to Gettysburg, Pennsylvania. I never could catch her at home. I tried a couple times to call her on the phone, but I don't like calling on the phone because sometimes you can't contact them or they turn you down and you don't get the chance to show the books. I called Ginger on the phone, and she told me to come the next day.

So I drove to her house, and she invited me in. She was a young lady about twenty-four years old, about the same age as my daughter at that time. Ginger was a sweet girl and had two little boys. We sat on the couch as I showed her the *Bible Stories,* and she just loved the books. She told me that when she was a little girl she would go into the doctor's office and read these books. Her mommy never bought the books for her, but she always wanted the books.

She decided she would get these books for her two little boys. As I closed and she decided to buy the books, she got out her checkbook, and I started to write up the contract. Then her husband walked in. I said a little prayer and jumped up to shake his hand and told him that Ginger sent the card in. I handed the card to him. He looked at her, and he looked at me, and he said, "What my wife wants, my wife gets."

We talked for a while, and I asked him what type of work he did. He did drywall work, which I did before I became a literature evangelist. When I finished writing up the contract for Ginger, she said, "You know why I want these books, Don? I'm dying of cancer. The doctors tell me I have about six months to live. I want to make sure my little boys are brought up on these books because I believe these books are very simple to understand and will help my children."

I couldn't believe she had only six months to live. She looked so healthy and so full of joy and love. I walked out of that home feeling very sad knowing that this young lady had such a short time to live. I shared the story with my wife and many nights we prayed for Ginger.

About three months later, I was going to Gettysburg so I stopped by to see Ginger. Her husband came to the door, and we talked for a while. Finally, I said, "How is Ginger doing?"

Then he told me that Ginger had died. She didn't even have six months. She only had a few months, but she got those *Bible Story* books for her little boys. I was really glad that I didn't give up on Ginger no matter how many times I went to her home and called her on the phone. The Holy Spirit wanted this young lady to have these books for her little boys to be brought up on God's Word. Thank God for these books; they change lives.

God Spared My Life

Dwight and Jessica lived in Waynesboro, Pennsylvania, and sent in a card. I tried two or three times to catch them at home. One day I was in the area, and I said a little prayer hoping this time I'd find them at home. Sure enough, when I knocked on the door, Dwight came to the door. I showed him the card, and he invited me in. As we sat on the couch, his wife, Jessica, walked in, and we started talking. I soon found out that she was a nurse and worked in Hagerstown, Maryland.

As I showed the books to them, Dwight fell in love with everything I presented him. He would ask if I had anything else. I reached into my case and showed him the *Bedtime Stories*. He loved them. They had a little girl. I showed them the *Bible Stories*. They wanted those. I showed them *Bible Friends, Forever Stories, The Desire of Ages*, and *Bible Readings for the Home*. At the end, Dwight decided they wanted to buy all the books I had, more than $1,000 worth of books. I wrote the contract up and gave them a few little paperback books.

Dwight said, "You don't have to give those to us."

I said, "Well, there's certain people in churches who give me money, and they say that when I find a family in need or who buys some books, I can also give them some books free."

He thought that was very nice and he told Jessica, "I think we should help Don." Then he wrote out another check, and when he handed me the check for the books he bought, he handed me a second check for $100 for me to use to buy literature to hand out to people who couldn't afford the books. They were the first family in my thirty-six years of working for God as a literature evangelist who gave me money to help buy books for someone else.

Then Dwight told me this story. He said, "I have a really bad back. It was broken in a car accident, and I can't work anymore. I'm on disability."

He told me this story. He was coming home one night with his truck, and on the trailer he was hauling a little Geo car. A car came straight at him, and it didn't get over to the side and hit him head-on. It went underneath his truck and the roof went up through the floorboard and pushed him up in the air and broke his back and busted his leg. He was in bad shape, and because of this accident, he can't work anymore. Dwight showed me the pictures and told me that the driver had come from a party where they were all drinking.

The young driver was thirty-four years old and died at the scene. The passenger in the front seat was thirty years old and also died immediately. There was a young man in the back seat who died in the hospital later; he was sixteen years old. Three young lives were plucked out that night from alcohol, and Dwight almost lost his life.

He was so glad to get these books for his little girl and be given a second chance.

The Gas Station

As I was running a lead card in Williamsport, Maryland, I knocked on some other doors in the area trying to find out where this address was. I then stopped at a gas station and asked the station attendant if he knew where 101 Sunset Avenue was. He said that was the address of the gas station. I asked if Mary was there. He said Mary wasn't there today but her husband was. I talked to her husband, and he told me that Mary would be in next week on Wednesday. So I set the appointment up and went to see Mary the next Wednesday.

She was a very nice lady and we had a great time visiting. As I was talking with Mary, a mechanic came out from the garage. Mary told him, "You need these books."

He said, "What kind of books are they?" I showed him *Bible Readings for the Home* and *The Great Controversy* and some children's books. He really liked what he saw and listened for about five or ten minutes. He went back to work, and I talked with Mary a little longer. She had no interest at the time, but I gave her some books, and she thanked me. The mechanic walked back out of the garage and asked how much the books were. After telling him the price, he decided to purchase the books.

As I walked out of that gas station, I thought about how this lady had sent a card in requesting information on the *Bible Stories* but that the mechanic who worked at the gas station was the one the Lord had intended for me to see. That's the way God works. He sets up the appointment before we even get there.

The Dog

I ran a lead card in Boonsboro, Maryland, one day. I knocked on the door and talked to the lady, but she told me this wasn't the right house and that it was her daughter across the street. She had sent the card in for her daughter because she had children.

I found the house and cautiously looked around because in the country they have something that you don't want to meet. Dogs! As I got out of the car, there was a dog. I picked my feet up as I walked to keep him from biting me. He was growling at me and snapping at me. I was very nervous that he was going to bite me.

Finally, I got to the door and rang the bell. I prayed that someone was home so I didn't have to fight with the dog going back to my car. The lady came to the door, and I showed her the card that her mom had sent in for her. She was interested but didn't let me in the door. The dog was right beside me growling at me as we talked. She decided to buy the books, but she told me her checkbook was in the car. She asked me to meet her at the car. The dog went inside the house, and I thought I had gotten rid of it.

I walked to her car, and suddenly the dog ran out of the house toward me. All I could do was say a little prayer that I wouldn't have to hurt the dog and that he wouldn't bite me. Just as he got to me, he stopped and started nibbling at my pant leg. As the lady was writing the check, the dog just kept nibbling at me. I tried to push him away, but he would come right back. Sweat rolled off my face because I was so scared. She gave me the check and called the dog to stay there with her. When I got to my car, I said a little prayer thanking God for protecting me. How many times He protects us, and we don't even know it.

Time is Running Out

Bill Fentress worked as a literature evangelist for forty-two years. Bill and I became really close friends when he worked in Pennsylvania, and for about a year he was my district leader. We had some great times together. When we became independent literature evangelists, we kept in touch with each other.

We encouraged and prayed for each other. Bill decided he would retire after his forty-two years of service. But before he did, he decided to try a different approach. He wrote up a letter and took the letter to the principals of the Mennonite schools and asked them to take the letter to their churches and let the people know that he wasn't going to be working in their area anymore and that they probably wouldn't be able to get the books anymore. He gave a two month period in which he would be working in the area yet. The response went very well. He sold several sets to the schools.

At one school he went to there were three teachers sitting outside. Bill walked up and introduced himself and explained what he was doing and asked if they would put the letter in their church. One of the young ladies said she would be glad to but would like to have the books for her home. She said she wasn't married but that she would probably get married in the future and would love to have the books for her children since she was brought up on the books. The other two young ladies sitting there with her told Bill that they also wanted to buy *The Bible Story* books. All three young unmarried teachers bought the books from Bill. You never know what is going to happen.

Picture on the Door

I was knocking on doors in a little town close to Hagerstown, Maryland, and it was getting dark out. However, I was driving by this house and saw a light on the door and there on the door hung one of our beautiful pictures of Jesus knocking at the door. I decided to knock on the door, and Mary opened it. I explained to her what I was doing, and she invited me in. As I was talking to Mary and her husband, I found out that they had bought some books from a literature evangelist years ago and had enjoyed the books very much.

As I showed her some of the other books we had available, they liked what they saw and made the decision to buy some of them. The interesting part of this story is that Mary and her husband take care of foster children, and she probably had about seven or eight children at her home at that time. But they don't just take care of foster children, they take care of handicapped foster children; children that no one else wants. Mary said they wanted to give them a good home and teach them about Jesus. What a beautiful family!

I went back two or three times more to see Mary, and every time she would buy more books from me to teach the children. She moved to a different location, and I still found Mary while knocking on doors. Then many months later, I was in the same area knocking on doors, and Mary had moved again. This time, I had no idea where she had moved to.

Then while I was knocking on some apartment doors, I saw a couple go into one of the apartments, and when I got down a little further, I found out it was Mary and her husband. If I hadn't seen her walk into her apartment, I would have bypassed her door because she wouldn't have been home.

I talked with her at the door, and she said she thought she had everything I sold. We just laughed, but there was a lady sitting on the couch who said that she didn't have my books. So Mary invited me in, and I showed her friend the books while Mary listened. As we talked, I found out that her friend, Cathy Williard, was related to me and lived close to where my parents lived. She looked in the back of the book and saw that the publisher was the Review and Herald.

She said, "I don't always agree with what these books say. Do you have anything else?" I showed her the health books, and she really liked those. She purchased those books. They were also published by the Review and Herald, but she bought them.

We had prayer together, and Mary told me that she had taken more than fifty handicapped foster children into her home throughout the years, and many of them she had adopted. God is using others to reach out to people and tell them the story of Jesus. Thank God for people like Mary who touch the lives of children.

The Fire

I was trying to find a person who sent in a card in Chambersburg, Pennsylvania. Down a long dirt road there was a trailer and a barn. No one answered when I knocked on the trailer door, so I started to go. About that time the farmer came over and talked to me and asked me what I wanted. I showed him the card his wife sent in requesting information on *The Bible Story* and *Bedtime Stories*. He told me his wife wasn't there but would be home in about an hour. He asked if I could come back, and I told him I would.

I decided to go to the store and get something to drink. I prayed that she would be home when I went back. Sure enough, there was a car at the trailer. I knocked on the door, and a lady came to the door. She invited me in to talk. She told me she had those books when her children were little. The children just loved them, and now that all three of her children were grown up and had children, they wanted those books now.

She told me that a couple of weeks ago they had gone out to eat dinner, and when they got back, their house was on fire and had burned to the ground. There was nothing left. They lost everything they had. She started crying because some of the things such as the pictures of the children when they were little were irreplaceable. She couldn't replace the books they had. She saw the card in the doctor's office and mailed it in hoping and praying that she could get the books back for her children.

I was showing her the *Bedtime Stories*, and she really wanted them. She told me how much her children loved the stories in those books and never forgot them. I told her that the books had been redone and that some of the stories weren't in the new set.

I had a new set in the car with me. She called her husband to ask about the new set and decided they would purchase it. I went out to get the books and opened the trunk and pulled out the box of *Bedtime Stories*. It was not the new set but the older set. I went back into the home and told her that I had the old set of books that she really wanted. She called her husband again and told him that I had the old set and was so excited about it. She thanked me for coming and said the children and grandchildren would love the books too. I thanked God again and again for letting me have the old set of *Bedtime Stories* with me.

The Letters

I get many letters sent from people telling me how much they appreciate these books. One letter stated:

> "Don, thank you for sharing with me how God has worked in your life with your ministry. Keep spreading the literature of Jesus. God bless you. These books have helped my children so much." — Linda

This is from a young lady, nineteen-year-old Amy who I met while knocking on doors in Hagerstown. At that time, she was going to college and didn't have money to buy the books. I told her I would give her the books if she would send me the money. The money came about a week later with a letter from Amy.

> "Dear Mr. Draper, I want to thank you for taking the time to stop by and educate me more on Christ, also for trusting me enough to send you the money in the mail. I pray that you will keep on touching people the way you touched me. Best of luck to you. Take care and God bless you." — Amy

Where God Leads

I was working near Shippensburg, Pennsylvania, where many Amish and Mennonite people lived. I was working with my district leader, and an Amish lady came to the door. She invited us in, and we talked with her about the books. She walked over to her bookshelf and pulled out *The Desire of Ages*. She hugged it to her heart as she said, "This book was inspired by God."

She purchased many books from us and loved our books. It made me feel so good to know that people feel so highly about these books. It shows us that God says the printed page is a powerful tool.

Another Mennonite family we met told me that they read the *Bedtime Stories* so many times that they wore the pages out and needed to buy another set of books. One Mennonite family gave me a list of more than 100 families to go see. Many of them purchased books and many of them already had our books. They love our material; they read those books. Many of those children's lives are changed. These books are a blessing to so many people.

The Lady
With Pictures

As I was canvassing on a back road in Pennsylvania, I saw in the yard of a home all kinds of statues of Jesus and pictures of the Bible hanging on the trees. I knocked on the door, and the lady invited me in. She had pictures of Jesus all over her walls. She just loved the Lord. As I showed her some of our books, she fell in love with them and purchased some of them from me. I went back to see Frances probably four or five times, and just about every time, she would purchase some books from me.

Time went by, and I hadn't been by to see Frances for about a year. I was in the area one day and went to see Frances. She told me a sad story. She said, "I thought about you the other day, and then you came to my door. A while back my children thought that I wasn't doing well so they put me in a nursing home and thought they'd get rid of me. But I got better, and when I came home, I was so disappointed because they had taken most of my furniture and sold it. They also took my money, and many of my books were gone. Everything they could sell in my home, they sold to make money. But I came home, and I'm here to stay. I found out that I don't have much time left, and I'm so glad you came."

She purchased some small books from me. We had prayer, and she cried and said, "I know I won't see you again in this life." We made a promise that nothing would keep us from wanting to be with our sweet Jesus in the kingdom.

A couple months later, I was in the area and stopped to see Frances. The house had been sold and all the beautiful statues in the yard were gone. Frances had passed away. I'm so glad that God has sent me to people such as Frances.

Working in
Apartments

I n the wintertime I decided to work in apartments. There were some very close to my house. One day I was knocking on doors, but before I started, I prayed, "Lord, don't let me go to the office." There were no soliciting signs everywhere, and I thought I would be asked to leave.

I went into the first apartment, and the office sign was there, but I didn't see it. I was on the bottom floor and about the third door down from the office. I knocked on a door and a tall young man answered. His name was James. As I was talking to James, I pulled out a book at the door and showed it to him. He asked me to come in. His girlfriend, Jewel, was sitting at the table. I sat down at the table with James and Jewel and showed them some of our books. They really liked everything, and we had a nice long talk. I found out that they didn't know much about the Bible, but they were really interested.

As I was writing up the contract, James told me that on Monday Jewel had lost her job, and James was working two jobs and on Tuesday, he lost one of his jobs. He said, "I was just back in my office praying and telling the Lord that I didn't know what to do when you knocked at my door. You were an answer to prayer. Because you were talking about God, I invited you in."

He said the books would be a blessing to Jewel and him because they were planning on being married soon.

I prayed with them and then asked if they would be interested in studying the Bible. They looked at each other and both said yes. I set up an appointment and began studying the *Amazing Facts study* guides with them.

One time I was studying with them and Treasure, Jewel's daughter, said to me,

"Do you know who my favorite Bible character is?"

I said, "No. Who?"

She said it was Moses. I asked her if she had ever heard the story of Queen Esther. She said she hadn't, and so I told her the story about Esther. James was listening, and he said, "Don, is that in the Bible?"

I said, "Yes, it is, James."

Then I told her the story of Daniel and his friends. Again, James stopped me and said, "Don, is that in the Bible?"

I said, "Yes, it is, James."

You see, so many people are out there who do not know much about the Bible. Many have never had the opportunity to read these stories in the Bible. God sends literature evangelists into homes to share these stories with people and put the books in homes so lives can be changed. I'm so glad that God sent me to see James and Jewel. They have been coming to church sometimes. I'm praying that the Holy Spirit will touch their hearts and lead them to know Jesus better.

The Apartment Next Door

As I was studying with James and Jewel, I decided to knock on some more apartments in that area. I knocked on a door on the bottom floor again, and a young lady answered. I told her what I was doing and showed her some of our books. She listened and then called her husband to come to the door. I was telling him about our books, and he stopped me and asked if I was a Seventh-day Adventist. I told him I was, and then he told me he was a member of the Seventh-day Adventist Church also.

He told me his wife was not. We talked a little longer and found out that we went to the same church. He told me his father would love to talk with me. He lives in Florida, but he had worked in Brazil as a literature evangelist for about ten or twelve years. God truly blessed him. He was telling his wife about the *Bedtime Stories* and the *Bible Friends*.

All of a sudden he said, " Sis, come here." His sister was visiting them, and he asked her if she remembered reading the *Bible Friends* when they were little. She started laughing and said yes she remembered how their father read those stories to them all the time.

God is always leading. You never know who you're going to meet and what experiences you will have. The angels go before us and touch the hearts. In Jeremiah 6:9 it says, "Be not afraid of their faces for I will put my words in your mouth."

God Will Help Our Literature Evangelists

I'd just like to share with literature evangelists how God has blessed me with help to buy literature. I go to churches and tell stories and at the end of my sermon, I make a call that if God has touched anyone I need their help. Many people would like to do more for the Lord but because of health or jobs they can't get out to their homes and visit people. But I tell them I can, and with the money given me, I buy literature to hand out. I have truck drivers who send me money every month and churches and others who come up to me and give me money after sermons. My prayer is that you will try this and watch God at work.

I've been in this work for more than thirty-six years, and I pray that I will be able to continue working until the Lord comes or until my life ends. I pray that I can help lead many souls to God. I'm a man with a burden—that's what "colporteur" means. When my mission ends and I get to heaven, I want to see all of the many precious souls who have come to God through this literature.

We are told to spread these books like the leaves of autumn. Read these books, dear friends; they are God's books. Hug them to your hearts, and thank God that we have literature we can read until the end of time!

As you've read these pages, perhaps you have realized that God has called you to be a literature evangelist—or to be a better mom or dad, a better grandparent, brother or sister, husband or wife, a better son or daughter. Whatever God has called you to be, do it with your heart. Put your whole heart into it. Claim the promise of James 1:5: "If any man lacks wisdom, let him ask of God, who upbraideth not, and it shall be given." Claim it, and go forward. Then when you look back, you can thank God for what He has done for you.

In closing, I'd like to say that if you've been impressed by this book and it has changed your heart, I pray that you will never again be the same. If you have read this book and God has touched your heart, I pray that you will remember to support literature evangelism.

I have people from everywhere send me money to support my ministry and to help me stay in the literature work. I go out there by faith that God will supply my needs. I buy thousands of dollars of literature a year to hand out free to those who need it but cannot afford it. The money people send me helps me buy that literature and keeps me in God's work. If God has touched you and you would like to help, I thank you in advance. Whatever you send will be a blessing in more ways than you can think of.

If we don't meet on this earth, may we meet in heaven. God bless you.

Don Draper
416 Chartrige Dr.
Hagerstown, MD 21742

We invite you to view the complete
selection of titles we publish at:

www.TEACHServices.com

Scan with your mobile
device to go directly
to our website.

Please write or email us your praises, reactions, or
thoughts about this or any other book we publish at:

TEACH Services, Inc.
P U B L I S H I N G
www.TEACHServices.com

P.O. Box 954
Ringgold, GA 30736

info@TEACHServices.com

TEACH Services, Inc., titles may be purchased in bulk for
educational, business, fund-raising, or sales promotional use.
For information, please e-mail:

BulkSales@TEACHServices.com

Finally, if you are interested in seeing
your own book in print, please contact us at

publishing@TEACHServices.com

We would be happy to review your manuscript for free.

CPSIA information can be obtained
at www.ICGtesting.com
Printed in the USA
JSHW060520131022
31617JS00003B/48

9 781572 589452